THERE *IS* A BETTER WAY TO LIVE.

Choice! The key is *choice*. You have options. You need not spend your life wallowing in failure, ignorance, grief, poverty, shame, and self-pity. But, hold on! If this is true then why have so many among us apparently elected to live in that manner?

The answer is obvious. Those who live in unhappy failure have never exercised their options for a better way of life because *they have never been aware that they had any choices!*

—From *The Choice*

Bantam Books by Og Mandino

THE CHOICE

OG MANDINO

BANTAM BOOKS
NEW YORK · TORONTO · LONDON · SYDNEY · AUCKLAND

THE CHOICE
A Bantam Book
Bantam hardcover edition / April 1984
A Selection of the Literary Guild of America
Bantam paperback edition / April 1986

ISBN 0-553-24576-7

Published simultaneously in the United States and Canada

Bantam Books are published by Bantam Books, a division of Bantam
Doubleday Dell Publishing Group, Inc. Its trademark, consisting of the
words "Bantam Books" and the portrayal of a rooster, is Registered in U.S.
Patent and Trademark Office and in other countries. Marca Registrada.
Bantam Books, 1540 Broadway, New York, New York 10036.

PRINTED IN THE UNITED STATES OF AMERICA

OPM   30   29   28   27   26   25   24   23   22

Dedicated to a beautiful lady who taught me the true meaning of love, many years ago . . . my sister, Jackie.

I am bigger than anything that can happen to me. All these things, sorrow, misfortune, and suffering, are outside my door. I am in the house and I have the key.

CHARLES FLETCHER LUMMIS

Man is made or unmade by himself. By the right choice he ascends. As a being of power, intelligence, and love, and the lord of his own thoughts, he holds the key to every situation. . . .

JAMES ALLEN

THE CHOICE

I

THE ONLY CALENDAR I NEED IS JUST OUTSIDE MY WINDOW. Maple leaves, in the trees on my hill, have now turned pallid and brittle, their lush reds and golds drained by the brutish frosts of the past week.

"Do your work well and then be ready to depart when God shall call," wrote a great nineteenth-century wise man, Tyron Edwards. Both his words and the analogy of the leaf completing its life cycle weigh heavily on my mind as I sit alone, here in my studio, and pray for the strength to cope with my terrible secret.

Within ninety days I expect to be dead.

I am writing this narrative as swiftly as I can because, in truth, I have no idea how much time, how much living, remains for me. Will I make it to Thanksgiving? Maybe. To Christmas? Very doubtful. But for a certainty the inevitable snow that will soon cover every fallen leaf will also blanket my grave before the new year has counted many days.

Am I being ravaged by some malignant disease? No. Only four months ago, after my annual checkup, Dr. Scagno assured me that all systems were "go" and that I inhabited one of the healthiest forty-two-year-old bodies he had examined in a long time.

Am I planning to take my own life? God forbid. If ever a man had everything to live for, that person is me.

So why this terrible sense of impending doom, this certainty of a deadline (such an apt word) on my life that has triggered this hasty recital on the typewriter. After all, who among us has any guarantee that he or she will even see tomorrow's sunrise? Perhaps by the time you finish reading these words you will understand.

Hopefully, by the time I complete these brief memoirs, if I finish, I, too, will have a much better perspective of all that has happened to me since that memorable morning, more than six years ago, when I suddenly changed the direction of my life. The decision was mine and mine alone, you must understand, and even with my days now limited, I would do it all again if life had such a thing as reruns.

Every day all of us make hundreds of choices, most of them so menial and habitual that they are almost as automatic as breathing. What we have for breakfast, the clothes we wear, the route we take to work, the bills we pay or lay aside, the television programs we watch, the functions of our job, the manner in which we greet friend or foe, none of these is memorable beyond the hour.

But there are other choices we must make from time to time, decisions that we can later look back on from any age plateau and recall with bitter sadness or triumphant joy depending on how they affected the years that followed. Rarely are these momentous turning points in life ever planned or expected. How can they be when the vast majority of humans wander along the pathway of years without any destination or goal or even a road map?

Since so many don't know where they are, or where they're going, they are always struggling merely to survive, always on the razor's edge of disaster, forever on the defensive. When one must live that way, one's options are limited.

Not me! Not Mark Christopher, Treasury Insurance Company's youngest resident vice-president, responsible for eighty-four branch offices throughout New England and the sales production of more than seven hundred salesmen, saleswomen, and sales managers. Not Mark Christopher who was also an adjunct assistant professor at Northeastern University, teaching classes one night a week, whenever I was not traveling, on *Salesmanship*.

Truly, my future was unlimited. If my region continued to lead the company in sales volume, as it had for four straight years, a promotion to the home office in Chicago was inevitable. I can still remember the glowing letter of praise I received from J. Milton Hadley, founder and still president of Treasury Insurance, after he had read the flattering profile piece on me that had appeared in *The Boston Globe*. In that lengthy and illustrated article the writer had tagged me with a nickname that I've lived with ever since—"Mr. Success."

Whenever I delivered a speech at any of our sales conventions, I was always quoting passages from books by the greatest self-help writers and exponents of success. And for Christmas, as well as birthdays, every person in every branch office under my supervision could count on receiving an inspirational or success book from me that I was certain would help his or her career—books by people such as Napoleon Hill, Franklin Bettger, Dorothea Brande, Maxwell Maltz, W. Clement Stone, and Norman Vincent

Peale. "Mr. Success" was an appropriate handle, I thought, for someone who knew exactly what his goals were and where to find the answers on how to achieve them.

And then, on a morning I shall never forget, I began a new life. It had been like hundreds of other predawn Sundays stretching back through the years. At the first noisy eruption from my alarm clock I awoke and quickly flipped the off button before it disturbed Louise. I slipped quietly from bed and walked to the window. A rain storm promised on last night's television news had not materialized. The stars were still out, and a thin quarter moon was only now wearily retreating down behind the trees. This was going to be a perfect summer day, New England at its best.

I showered, shaved, and dressed in my favorite golf outfit, the Arnold Palmer shirt with matching beige slacks that had set me back ninety bucks at the pro shop, and tip-toed downstairs to the kitchen.

While the water was heating for my cup of instant coffee I went out into the garage, touched the button on our electric garage door opener, stepped carefully between the bicycles and two automobiles, and hauled my golf clubs out onto the driveway. Usually they were stored in my locker at the country club, but I had just returned, on Thursday, from a life underwriter's gathering in Bermuda and had managed to get in a little golf at the course adjoining our hotel, the Southampton Princess. Now, when the guys came by I'd be ready. Tee-off time for us at the club, as it had been every Sunday for years, was seven sharp.

I downed my orange juice and my two One-a-Day vitamin pills and sat with my coffee and doughnut. I had at least twenty minutes before I would hear the single toot from the station wagon carrying the rest of the foursome.

As I sipped my coffee I watched a flock of robins careening recklessly around a large maple tree in the corner of our backyard. Occasionally, on some mysterious signal, they would all halt their race and settle on the lowest bough of the tree, each tiny bird equidistant from the next, each respecting the other's territory, something we humans have forgotten how to do. At rest or in flight, however, their raucous chirpings combined to produce a din, in the stillness of the morning, that would have done credit to any low-budget horror movie.

Then I heard something else—the sound of bare feet in the upstairs hallway. The kitchen clock read 6:15. Who was up? Soon I heard a second set of feet. Could both boys be having bathroom call at the same time? Possible.

My mind returned to the match coming up. I had played terribly last week, but today was going to be different. I was positive. I had straightened out that wild hook of mine in Bermuda, and now I was ready. I let my body relax and began practicing the art of "picturization" that I had learned from so many of the masters of success, through their books. Simple technique. You merely picture in your mind having already accomplished or attained your goal, whatever it may be. Hold it firmly in your thoughts, picture it as already being yours, and amazing things will happen. That simple process, through the years, has paid off for me on much more important objectives than correcting a golf swing.

I was still mentally working on my drives, my back to the hall that leads from the upstairs stairway, so I didn't see them when they came up behind me. But I heard them, my two sons. In unison they said, "Happy Father's Day, Dad!" Then I was embraced as only a twelve-year-old and a six-year-old can manhandle you, and each kissed my cheek.

Todd, my youngest, was holding a white envelope on which he had written, "Dad." He handed it to me with all the pride he usually reserved for an "A" school paper. I opened the envelope and carefully removed the card, which read, "To the Greatest Father in the World." It was signed with the same large and undisciplined scrawl, "love, Todd."

Then my twelve-year-old, obviously feeling a little too grown-up for such sentimental foolishness, handed me his envelope. His card was exactly like Todd's—"To the Greatest Father in the World." Todd, before his older brother could shush him, said, "We bought them with our own money, Dad!"

I hugged and kissed them both, telling them how thoughtful they had been to remember. After a few minutes of small talk, Todd yawned, and I suggested that they both get back to bed since it was very early. They wouldn't even consider it. They had planned to see me before I left for the course and now that they were up they were going to remain up. Soon they were at the table, giggling and devouring large helpings of the latest obscenely colored, vitamin-enriched cereal.

As I watched and listened to the two of them, a strange feeling came over me. Perhaps it was no more than an illusion created by the early morning mist seeping through the screen door, but Glenn, my twelve-year-old, seemed to be aging before my eyes. Or maybe it was just the first time I had taken a good look at him since I couldn't remember when. He was handsome and, luckily for him, was getting to look more and more like his mother. Gosh he had grown up. There was even a hint of fuzz above his upper lip; his hands seemed immense, and his voice had a break in it. Between my long hours at the office and university plus my weekends on the golf course,

I hadn't noticed his gradual transition from the infant I once bathed every night to the young man who now sat before me. The horrible thought suddenly hit me that he would be off to college in five years and more or less out of my life in ten.

I turned my attention to Todd who was struggling to read aloud from the back of his giant cereal box. He was already in the first grade. It was only yesterday, wasn't it, that I had paced the floor outside the delivery room until I heard his first cry? Where did those six years go? He glanced up from his bowl, and all I could see were those big brown eyes, cloned directly from his mother. For the first time I noticed how red his hair had become—almost the shade of his grandmother's hair, which he had never seen and never would see. My mother would have loved and spoiled these two.

Todd returned my stare with a frown. "What's the matter, Dad, don't you like the cards?"

I assured him that they were great, the very best Father's Day cards I had ever seen. Then I heard the horn. The guys had arrived. I stood, gave them both another hug, and headed toward the garage. They followed me. When I reached the driveway, Todd said, "Play a good game!" and Glenn shouted, "I hope you win!"

I waved and walked down the driveway toward the awaiting car. Bob leaped out of the driver's side to open the back gate in his station wagon for my golf clubs. I said "Good morning" and a few other words. Bob frowned, angrily shook his head, and got back in the car, slamming the door. He gunned the motor and roared off.

I stood there in my Arnold Palmer shirt with pants to match hardly comprehending what I had done. Watching me from the garage, as puzzled as I was, stood my two pajama-clad boys.

Finally, Todd came running down the driveway and leaped into my arms. I buried my face in his small chest until he pushed my head back and asked, "Daddy, why are you crying?"

What could I say to him?

How could I tell him that my tears were for all those hours and days and years I had spent on all the projects and sales meetings and golf courses that would still be there long after my two little men became big men and left me forever?

II

ON THE FOLLOWING MORNING I DICTATED MY LETTER OF resignation, with thirty days notice, to J. Milton Hadley. Four days later, just as I expected, I answered the phone in my office and heard a familiar voice.

"Mark, what's going on?"

"Hi, Martha, how's the greatest executive secretary in the country?"

"Never mind how I am. What's wrong with you?"

"Nothing. I'm terrific. Feel like the weight of the world is off my shoulders, and I never realized how heavy it was until I unloaded it."

"Mr. Hadley read your letter."

"And? . . ."

"He would like to meet with you, out at the mansion, as soon as possible."

"I thought so, but it won't do any good. I've made up my mind."

"Mark, you don't have to convince me! I know you better than he does. I've been trying to get you to change your mind about a few other matters for more than five years. God! The unflappable, indomitable, incorruptible Mr. Christopher! But he still would like to see you—at your convenience, of course."

"Of course. Where is he?"

"In L.A. for a speech to the American Bankers Association, but he'll be back late tonight."

"How's his schedule tomorrow?"

"Full, as always. But there's nothing on it that can't be cancelled."

"Okay, I'll be there around noon. My secretary will call you back with my arrival time as soon as she firms up my airline reservation."

"The limo will be waiting for you at O'Hare."

"Fine."

"Mark?"

"Yes, Martha?"

"You damn fool!" The line went dead.

J. Milton Hadley's huge teakwood-paneled library encompassed an entire wing of his twenty-eight-room estate on a small rise overlooking Lake Michigan. Why he called it his library was a mystery to everyone since there was not a single book in sight except for a large, leather-covered Bible that was supposed to have been George Washington's very own. Mr. Hadley was not a "reader," he would explain to those he considered important enough to allow into this inner sanctum, he was a "doer."

The man himself was seated at his huge Oriental hand-carved desk directly beneath a life-size oil portrait of Dwight Eisenhower in his general's uniform. Mr. Hadley, it was said, had been Ike's largest campaign contributor in his two successful runs for the Presidency, and he had been offered the ambassadorship of Italy for his favors but declined, claiming that he didn't like pasta or opera and would have been bored to death in Rome within three months.

Seated to the left of Mr. Hadley's desk was Morris Rosen, Treasury Insurance Company's vice-president and general counsel, looking as harried as ever, and on his right was Wilbur Gladstone, vice-president and comptroller. After I shook hands all around, Mr. Hadley gestured to the empty seat facing him and the others—making me a perfect cross-fire target for all three of them.

The old man was never one for small talk. He leaned forward, adjusted his gold-rimmed glasses, and cleared his throat.

"Mark, you are one of our company's greatest assets. I have always said that our wealth and our strength lies not in our investments but in people like you, heroes on the firing line day after day. You have performed miracles in the twelve years you have been with us, and you are still such a young man. Amazing! I'm very proud of you. Last year your region produced almost a billion dollars of new insurance coverage, and the turnover of salespeople under your supervision is probably the lowest in the industry. You were made for this business, and I just hate to see all your years of hard work and dedication tossed aside."

He rummaged impatiently through a small pile of papers on his desk and finally held up my letter of resignation, waving it as if it were a fan. "Your letter states no reason for your wanting to leave our company. I feel, at the very least, you owe me an explanation. Would you mind telling us, here in private, just what has brought about this sudden decision, assuming that it is a sudden decision?"

During my flight from Boston I had tried to anticipate all the questions I might be asked and jotted down my answers on a legal pad, changing them, refining them, rewording them until they satisfied me. But it was different now, sitting before this great genius of a man whom I respected so much, a man who had built a company valued at more than two billion dollars in less than fifty years and whose accomplishments filled two full columns in *Who's Who in America.*

I forced myself to look directly into his eyes. "Sir, ever since joining this company I have devoted nearly all my waking moments toward the advancement of my career, moving from one challenge to the next as if it all were a game, a game I was positive I could win. Only recently has it dawned on me that the losers in my game, the way I was playing it, were the three people who love me and need me the most, my wife and sons. The price they have had to pay, through the years, has been too damn high."

Mr. Hadley frowned and ran his finger down a pink sheet on the top of his pile. "But it appears to me, Mark, that you are quite able to reward their sacrifices and attend to all their needs in a way that would be the envy of ninety-nine percent of this country's population."

I shook my head. "I'm afraid you don't understand, Mr. Hadley. My decision has little to do with money but everything to do with time. When my oldest son played his first Little League game, where was I? Up in Portland conducting a sales meeting. When my youngest son challenges me to a game of Ping-Pong or wants to toss a football around, what do I usually tell him? That I'm too busy or too tired, but we'll do it tomorrow, for sure. Well, I've just awakened to the fact that I don't have any guaranteed tomorrows. None of us do. When my wife was in her terrible automobile accident, it took them seven hours to locate me because I was out in the New Hampshire countryside, field training a new manager. Do you know, I can count on the fingers of one hand the dinners I've had with all my family in the last twelve months, excluding this past week? Those three beautiful people don't have a father and a husband! What they have is a money-machine that drops in now and then, changes its clothes, and leaves again. They deserve more, and so do I. While I still can, I'm going to take a crack at smelling those roses that everyone keeps talking about."

Morris Rosen, general counsel, had been scribbling furiously on his stenographer's pad. He raised his pen and said, "But isn't some of your problem because of your own priorities regarding your free time? Don't you also teach in a university back there? That's time away from your family that has nothing to do with Treasury Insurance."

"You're correct, Morris. And I also play a lot of golf on Saturdays and Sundays. That's off my list, too, as well as my teaching. I'm going to stop this silly rat race I've managed to get myself into, count the blessings I already have, and let the rest of you keep running in your non-stop marathon to the rainbow. There must be a better way to live, and I'm going to drop out and see if I can find it."

Mr. Hadley sighed. "Eloquent words, Mark, but don't forget that even Thoreau finally had to come out of the woods. Didn't your kind of thinking go out with the sixties? Seems to me that people are trying to drop in, these days, not drop out. I take it that you are financially independent enough so that the risk is minimal in making such a drastic change in your life?"

"No sir, far from it. Louise and I never worried much about tomorrow, and so we've always lived just within my income. I imagine we have about thirty thousand dollars in stocks and savings accounts, and that's it."

Mr. Hadley smiled for the first time. "Isn't that an unusual financial condition for someone who has built such a marvelous career on convincing others that they should put away some of their earnings, through insurance and annuities, for rainy days?"

I smiled back. "Perhaps, but I've always felt I could deal with rainy days, when they came, better than most. I don't even own an umbrella."

His smile faded. "But of course you'll collect a sizeable amount when you cash in your pension and profit-sharing plans."

"I'm afraid not. I borrowed on both of them, as much as I could get, last year. My dad had two serious heart attacks, and he was hospitalized for almost five months. That plus the two specialists and the many private nurses he needed wiped out both my pension and profit-sharing nest eggs."

"And how is your father?"

"Dead, sir. We lost him last December."

"I'm sorry . . . and forgive all these personal questions. I'm asking only because I truly care about you. How about your home? Is there a large equity there?"

"No, sir. In building Treasury's New England region, state by state, we've had to move seven times. This house we live in now, in Brookline, is the first we've ever owned, and that's only been for the past two years. When we bought it we put down only the minimum payment, and if we sell it, we'll be lucky to come out even, considering what's happened to the real estate market."

Mr. Hadley leaned forward and frowned at an open file folder on his desk. "How does er-r-r-r Louise feel about this decision of yours?"

"Frankly, sir, she doesn't believe I'll go through with it. When I left her at the airport she was positive that after my meeting with you I'd change my mind, but she's hoping I won't. She's been my cheerleader for a long time, and she's with me all the way, although she did dig up an old line to remind me that although she had married me for better or worse, she wasn't sure that included for breakfast, lunch, and dinner."

"You have two sons, Mark?"

"Two great kids."

"And I imagine you expect to send them to college when the time comes?"

I knew I was being worked over by an expert. I also loved the man, and there was no sense fencing with him. I merely nodded.

Mr. Hadley rubbed his forehead for several minutes. "I must have missed something, son. You're only thirty-six. You've got at least that many more years ahead of you and most of them can be very productive ones. You're also, I know, a rational and brilliant man, and that's what's confusing me. Here you are with a total net worth that will only cover your family's living expenses for a couple of years, at the most, if all four of you cut way back on your lifestyle. Treasury Insurance has been your life and your career, a well-paying one, for many years. How are you going to support your family? Just exactly what is it that you are planning to do with the rest of your life?"

I hesitated, certain that if I told him my plan I would probably be greeted by uncontrollable laughter from all three. Mr. Hadley misread my silence and probably figured that this was the ideal moment for his thunderbolt. He rose, walked around the desk and placed his hand on my shoulder.

"Mark, Sam Larson, as you know, has been ailing for some time. He has now requested early retirement, and we have agreed. I am offering you his position as vice-president in charge of sales for the entire company at more than double your current income, including bonuses, and you can begin immediately. Of course you will have to move your lovely family here to the Chicago area and be prepared to put up with me almost every day, but I think we can both survive that. Please understand. This is not a sudden decision on our part. We have been aware of Sam's condition for some time, and your replacing him has already been discussed at two board meetings. All your letter of resignation has done is force us to move a little faster than we had planned. What do you say?"

What could I say? I was stunned. From the day I had made my first policy sale as a rookie salesman this had been my goal: to lick those seemingly impossible odds and climb to the top of the pile. Power, more money than I could ever spend, plus that inside track to one day possibly heading up the most progressive and profitable insurance company in the world. Morris and Wilbur were both smiling and nodding in tandem, leaning forward with anticipation.

"Now, Mark," Mr. Hadley continued, patting my shoulder. "You don't have to give me your decision today. I'm sure you'll want to talk this over with Louise and consider . . ."

He paused because I was shaking my head. "I don't have to talk it over with Louise, sir. She told me at the airport that whatever I decided would be okay with her, even if I changed my mind. But I haven't changed my mind, Mr. Hadley. I thank you for the wonderful offer, and I am honored, but I must decline."

The old man hastily removed his hand from my shoulder and returned to his seat. Morris and Wilbur sat staring down at their shoes. Mr. Hadley began tapping his pen against a large marble ashtray, his eyes resting on a silver-framed sepia print standing on the corner of his desk—an old faded photograph of himself and the late Mrs. Hadley and their four children.

Finally, he said softly, "Well, I can't give you very high grades for practical common sense; however, I do admire your courage. But tell me, because you didn't answer this one before. What will you do with yourself and all that free time? How do you plan to provide for those who depend on you? How are you going to fill the rest of your life?"

None of the three laughed when I told him. Instead, they all looked as if they had just heard me announce that I was planning to dive from the top of the John Hancock Building in the morning.

My declaration of independence was brief. With as much bravado as I could muster I said, "I'm going to become a writer!"

III

FOLLOWING THAT PAINFUL PARTING IN MR. HADLEY'S library, Louise and I made another major shift in our life's course, one that undoubtedly convinced even our closest friends and relatives that neither one of us was playing with a full deck any longer.

We bought a lighthouse!

Louise and I were on our second cups of coffee one morning, after Todd and Glenn had gone off to school, when the phone rang. Bob Boynton, Treasury Insurance Company's branch manager in Keene, New Hampshire, was on the line. Bob and I had become close friends during the past five years, although he was at least twenty years my senior in age and marketing experience. What I had liked most about Bob was that, despite my relative youth, there had never been a patronizing edge in his voice whenever he called me boss. Bob always ran a tight ship, and his sales increases, year after year, consistently placed his territory near the top in our region.

"Mark, I sure do miss you," said the gruff voice.

"I miss you too, Bob. How's it going?"

"Just great. Looks like we had another record year, up here."

"I wouldn't expect anything else from you."

"Mark, are you and Louise still house hunting?"

"Are we ever! You name any city or town in northern New England and I guarantee you we've been there in the past three months. I'll bet we've logged at least ten thousand miles but we still haven't found what we want at a price that we can afford. You know Louise. She keeps saying that when we see the place that's destined for us, we'll know it."

"Have you sold that house of yours?"

"We've not only sold it; we've passed papers. Lucky for us the buyer is an IBM executive being transferred from Dallas, but he's not moving in until the first of February. That gives us only three months before we've got to get out. We're paying him rent until then but it's getting close to panic time around here."

"Well, you can relax, old buddy, because I've found your next home. It's about fifteen miles from here, between the small towns of Jaffrey and Jaffrey Center. When you and Louise see it, you'll both know that your search has finally ended."

"What are you doing, a little real estate hustling on the side?"

"You must be kidding! When? From midnight to dawn? Are you familiar with the name, Joshua Croydon?"

"I've heard the name, Bob, but I can't put a handle on it."

"Well, Mark, Joshua Croydon was a brilliant naturalist,

and his children's books on the wonders of nature are the greatest."

"Of course. I think Todd has some of them. But what's Joshua Croydon have to do with . . ."

"Joshua Croydon died six weeks ago. He was seventy-nine. He was also a policyholder with Treasury Insurance, and I went out to his home near Jaffrey, yesterday, to help his widow complete the death claim forms. Their home is on top of a high hill about a quarter mile or so off Route 124. Comes with three acres of land, one of them always cultivated by Mr. Croydon for a garden. Both vegetables and flowers. Plus a small lawn. The rest of the hill is covered with maple trees and tall pines. The house is at least seventy years old and was built by an old whaling captain who once sailed out of Bath, Maine. Seven rooms. Four fireplaces. Original panels and woodwork inside. Completely insulated by the Croydons six years ago. White clapboard exterior and shake roof. There's also a big barn that they've used as a garage. Mrs. Croydon told me that she was going to put the place on the market. It's too much for her to manage, alone, at her age. I told her I thought I had a customer, and she promised to hold off calling the real estate people until I got back to her."

"How much? Did she say?"

"Ninety-five thousand. It's worth every cent of that, even in this depressed market. And that's not all. I've saved the best for last."

"Like every good salesman."

"No, no! Wait until you hear. Mark, were you serious when you announced, during that farewell party we threw for you at the Statler, that you were going to be a writer?"

"Dead serious."

"Well, listen to this. On the Croydon property, about thirty yards from their home, stands a lighthouse!"

"A what?"

"A lighthouse, maybe forty, fifty feet high."

"Bob, the Atlantic Ocean is at least sixty miles east of Jaffrey. What in God's name is a lighthouse doing in southwestern New Hampshire?"

"Beats me. Mrs. Croydon said that the original builder, that old sea captain, apparently wanted to erect some sort of monument to his glory days on those old schooners, and so, when he retired, he built himself a lighthouse. But, Mark, there's more. When the Croydons moved in, Joshua Croydon spared no expense to convert that lighthouse into his writing studio. You should see it! The interior, all the way up to the tower, is completely paneled in knotty pine, and in the center is a winding wrought iron stairway. And on the walls are bookshelves that one can reach from the circular stairway, enough bookshelves to handle all those books of yours!"

"It sounds almost too good to be . . ."

"Let me finish my sale's pitch. I've already told you that this place is on a hill. Well, when you climb those inside steps to the top of the lighthouse, you'll find a Thermopane enclosed tower room with lounge chairs and a table, instead of lanterns and high-powered beacons to guide lost ships. Stand up there in your own miniature heaven, and you have a view of Mount Monadnock, only six miles away, that will leave even you speechless. And you're up high enough so that on a clear day you can see some of the tallest peaks in Massachusetts and Vermont. The lighthouse even has its own fireplace and oil furnace. You can write out there all winter, as Mr. Croydon used to do. Mark, when you breathe that pine air and feel the peaceful quiet all around you, I guarantee that you'll reach for your checkbook! You owe it to yourself, and to Louise and the kids, to take a look at this gem."

The four of us did take a look, and it was love at first sight. We traded our two automobiles for a Jeep Wagoneer with four-wheel drive and arrived at our new home early in January, accompanied by two moving vans, one filled with more than a hundred cartons of my books. A station wagon was parked in front of the house, and as we turned up the circular driveway I saw Mrs. Croydon and another woman step from the car. She introduced us to her daughter who had come to help with the final packing and would drive the old lady to her new home, a small apartment near her other daughter's place in Nashua.

Mrs. Croydon seemed much more frail and tiny than the last time we had met, at the bank, and her voice broke frequently as she spoke. She smiled wistfully and said, "We just thought that we would wait a little while since you said you'd probably be here before noon. Somehow it didn't seem right to just leave the keys in the mailbox. It is much better that I personally turn them over to you, Mr. Christopher, and wish you and your lady and your beautiful children as much happiness, here, as Joshua and I were blessed with for more than thirty years."

Her hands were trembling when she placed the keys in mine. Then she turned and faced the front door, her thin shoulders visibly sagging. She shook her head. "There was no Joshua to hang a Christmas wreath on that door, last year. I don't know. I just don't know. How does one say farewell to the cradle of a thousand happy memories?"

She turned and embraced Louise who was fighting back tears. "Mrs. Christopher, please listen to an old woman. The years go by so swiftly. Enjoy each one, enjoy each day, and count your blessings. Never take them for granted. And I beg you, take good care of our home."

"We will, Mrs. Croydon," Louise sobbed, "we promise you."

The old lady glanced up at a blanket of dark clouds that now seemed to hover only a few yards above the hilltop. "We are moving none too soon. I smell snow. Oh—oh—I almost forgot! Come with me, Mr. Christopher. This won't take very long."

She grasped my hand and walked me toward the barn. As we stepped through the open doors into the musty shadows, she pointed toward a dark corner. "There you will find a snow-blower that will come in very handy up here. It is just two winters old, and it is yours. Also, there is the problem of plowing our long driveway that leads up to the house from Route 124. I recommend that you call a gentleman in Jaffrey whose name is Bill Lang. His number is in the phone book. He is kind and he is honest, and you can make arrangements with him to plow you out whenever it is needed—and believe me, it will be needed."

I thanked her. She took my hand again. "Now, let us go to the lighthouse for just a moment."

The lighthouse door was unlocked. She pushed down on its handle and led me inside. The sound of our footsteps echoed noisily against the pine walls, their bookshelves now stripped of Mr. Croydon's collection. All the other furniture and lamps had been removed from the ground floor except for a huge pine desk on which sat a rather ancient looking Underwood typewriter.

Mrs. Croydon's faint voice reverberated up through the lighthouse. "I understand that you are a writer, Mr. Christopher."

"I hope to be."

"It is a most difficult and lonely profession, and yet my husband's happiest hours, I am sure, were spent right here, sitting at that desk, surrounded by his books and struggling to find the correct words to describe, to his young readers, what his beliefs were concerning the true relationship between God and nature and man."

She leaned over the typewriter, and her fingers caressed the worn keys. "Late in the evening," she sighed, "whenever Joshua was working on a book, I would always bring him a pot of hot tea, out here, before I went to bed. He would break his concentration just long enough to thank me and kiss me good-night, and as I was going out the door I would always say the same words, 'Break a leg!' I was on the stage, many years ago, Mr. Christopher, and that is the strange manner in which actor people wish each other good luck."

I nodded. "Yes, I know. And tell me, Mrs. Croydon, what is the significance of all those pennies taped to the side of the typewriter?"

"Ah, yes," her face lit up. "Every time Joshua finished a book, he would tape another penny to his machine. There should be fourteen there. He said those were his copper notches, each signifying another small victory in his battle against intolerance and ignorance."

"I know I would have liked him. And will you be sending someone for his desk and typewriter?"

"Oh, no! They belong here. They are as much a part of this haven of peace as is that glass tower above. Permit me, please, to make you a gift of both, and may you be blessed with as much productive work and inner satisfaction, sitting there, as Joshua enjoyed."

On an impulse I opened my arms, and she leaned into them. I could feel her small body trembling. Finally, she looked up at me, biting on her lower lip, and whispered, "Break a leg, Mr. Christopher."

IV

BY EARLY MARCH WE HAD SETTLED IN PRETTY WELL. TODD and Glenn quickly learned exactly how long they could linger over breakfast before racing down the hill in time to be picked up by Mr. Flannery and his yellow school bus, and each day, after they were gone, Louise and I tackled another of the seemingly endless but necessary projects that always follow a moving.

Later, after Louise began her daily runs back and forth to Keene in search of new drapes and the hundreds of other household items that every male takes for granted, I began unpacking my cartons of books and arranging them on the lighthouse shelves. When they were all finally in place, the more than three thousand volumes were an impressive sight in their colored jackets, soaring in diminishing circles all the way up the tower's interior.

The lower shelves, those I could reach while standing on the rough granite floor, were reserved for my favorite and most valuable volumes on the subject of success and how to achieve it. In the past ten years, thanks to an antiquarian book dealer I discovered on Boston's Beacon Street, I had managed to accumulate more than 70 first editions, including Henry Ward Beecher's *Lectures to Young Men*, Samuel Smile's *Self-Help*, Horatio Alger's *Ragged Dick*, Russell Conwell's *Acres of Diamonds*, Dale Carnegie's *How to Win Friends and Influence People*, Alexander Anthony's *How to Conquer Life*, and Norman Vincent Peale's *The Power of Positive Thinking*.

Long before the last carton was emptied, I began work on my book, happily insulated from the outside world by the sweet-smelling pine walls of my lighthouse and the three feet of drifting snow outside. Within a few days I had mastered Joshua Croydon's cranky old Underwood and was punching out words at a respectable pace thanks to a course in typing I had taken, at my mother's insistence, during my senior year in high school. Typing, it seems, is one of those skills that once acquired is never forgotten, like riding a bicycle or swimming.

My mother. Perhaps it was no more than the reunion of my fingertips with typewriter keys after so many years, but memories of her and my early youth repeatedly intruded on my concentration during those initial days of solitary writing.

A freckle-faced Irish lass, with dark auburn hair and green eyes, Mother had me convinced as far back as I could remember that someday I would be a writer. "And not just a writer," she would always add with great bursts of enthusiastic faith, "but a *great* writer!" Where or how this zealous dream for her only son originated I never questioned, and I cooperated in every way, not only to please her but because I enjoyed listening to her vivid descriptions of the wonderful life I could lead when I became a famous author. She had me reading Kipling and Emerson while my playmates were still struggling with "Dick and Jane," and I was writing short stories with O'Henry-like endings, for her entertainment and mine, long before my classmates were forced to agonize over their first English composition.

Midway through my final year of high school our plans were set. I had applied to and been accepted by the University of Missouri, since both Mother and I agreed, after studying hundreds of college catalogs, that they had the finest school of journalism in the country. My father, bless him, always sat quietly by with a proud twinkle in his eyes as he watched and listened to the two of us chart my future.

And then, six weeks after I graduated from high school, my mother's brave heart stopped beating. No advance warning. One moment she was making a tuna-salad sandwich for my lunch and the next—she lay dead at my feet. No last words. Nothing.

Our dream was buried with her. Unable to handle what fate had dealt me, and despite all my father's tearful pleadings, I abandoned all thoughts of college and a writing career and eventually entered the field of sales, where I had prospered until two pajama-clad boys bearing Father's Day cards helped me to reevaluate my life.

Writing, I am convinced, is the least appreciated of all the creative arts. Only a miniscule portion of the population engages in sculpting or painting or composing but everyone writes—whether it be letters, invitations, shopping lists, or even just a signature on a check. It is not farfetched, therefore, for anyone with a smattering of self-esteem to believe that if he or she had the time, and the desire, an acceptable book or article could be produced.

A conservative estimate would be that, on any given

day or night in the United States alone, at least half a million individuals are involved in the process of writing a book. Each year more than forty thousand new works are actually published, and yet the sad truth is that only a handful of these ever attain sufficient sales to be profitable to both publisher and author. Is writing an easy road to fame and fortune? Hardly. A recent survey conducted for the Authors Guild Foundation revealed that the median annual income for a large segment of published authors was less than five thousand dollars!

Fortunately, I was not aware of these frightening statistics as I labored each day over Joshua Croydon's old Underwood. I knew what I wanted to write, and I tackled my project with a vengeance. My premise was a simple one. I believed then, and still do, that the tremendous growth of our nation during its first century and a half was due in great measure to the motivation and guidance provided by a unique group of individuals who wrote and lectured and often preached on success and how to achieve it. In each succeeding generation every child was exposed to the American dream at its best, at school and at home, through the works of Cotton Mather, Benjamin Franklin, Elbert Hubbard, Russell Conwell, Horatio Alger, Napoleon Hill and so many others.

In the second half of this century things changed. For the worse. As we began to grow fat and complacent, the voices of the old success apostles soon became little more than faint cries in the wilderness, all but drowned out by an unending parade of noisy hucksters peddling books, tapes, and seminars that are "certain" to earn you boundless wealth or propel you into the executive suite, sometimes in thirty days or less. Like fad diets, these swift and easy solutions to any problem, these quick fixes, soon sink into the oblivion they deserve when they are tried and found wanting.

In my book I intended to resurrect the old and forgotten success principles, techniques for achievement that had worked so well for past generations and been so effective for me. Working from my notes, which Louise had saved from all my sales convention speeches, plus the sourcebooks written by the true masters of success in my lighthouse library, the book slowly and painfully began to take on a meaningful shape and direction. I had carefully prepared a thorough outline covering all the enduring laws of success I wanted to deal with, and I allocated a chapter to each. Each chapter was written, edited, and rewritten, time and time again, page by page, sentence by sentence, often word by word. Agonizing work. Thoughts and concepts, so clear in my mind, often seemed confusing and pointless on paper. Rewrite. Do it again. And again. I would not compromise. Every chapter had to be strong enough to stand on its own, instructive, and above all, entertaining. There were already enough dull books on success and how to achieve it.

Writing a book, I quickly discovered, was on a far different dimension than preparing and delivering a speech. When a chapter was finally completed to my satisfaction, I heard no applause, received no pats on the back, no cheers, no standing ovations, no compliments on a job well done. What a lonely profession! With no feedback or encouragement, the motivation all had to come from within and had to be strong enough to overcome all the terrible pangs of self-doubt, insecurity, and even fear that were never far from the surface. I had to push on, had to believe that I would succeed because for me there was no retreat, no looking back. J. Milton Hadley and Treasury Insurance were certainly not waiting to pick me up and brush me off if I stumbled, and the future of the three most important people in my life rested now, more than ever, in my hands. I inched forward, chapter by chapter, week by week, month by month. The working title of my book was neither intended to be provocative nor especially commercial. I called it simply *A Better Way to Live*.

Despite my daily writing sessions in the lighthouse, I never allowed myself to forget the prime reason why I had walked away from the corporate rat race, to be with my family and to smell the roses. Together we cultivated and planted Joshua Croydon's old garden and thrilled at the appearance of every seedling of corn as much as if we had struck oil on that hilltop. When our first tomato was ripe enough to pluck, I remember carrying it into the house as if it were the Kohinoor Diamond, and the early cucumbers and lettuce made the most delicious salad we had ever eaten. I also volunteered to coach Todd's Little League team.

On weekends, and often in the afternoon when the boys returned from school, I would abandon my typewriter, and the four of us would pile into the Jeep Wagoneer with our road maps in search of another experience to share among the endless wonders of New Hampshire. What precious memories!

We swam in the ocean at Hampton Beach, rented a sailboat and rode the wind on Lake Sunapee, watched the harness races and ate cotton candy at the Hopkinton Fair, climbed to the top of Mount Washington on the Cog Railway, tossed coins in the wishing well at Santa's Village, gazed in awe at Hawthorne's immortal "Great Stone Face" crowned with snow, sailed a diesel steamer around the islands of Lake Winnipesaukee, and knelt to pray before the huge stone altar at the Cathedral of the Pines. To have a happy family, a wise man once wrote, is to enjoy an earlier heaven.

I had learned very early in my selling career that merely to have goals without a plan and a time limit was as useless as having no goals at all. My goal had been to complete the book in ten months, allowing two weeks for each of twenty chapters. I missed. By plenty. The final page of *A Better Way to Live* wasn't written until just after Thanksgiving, 1978, nearly twenty months after I had begun! Louise then took over, checking every page for grammatical and typographical errors before typing the final clean copy for me, with two carbons.

On one of our trips to Concord we had purchased the latest edition of *Writer's Market*, a hefty volume that annually catalogues American publishers, their current editors' names, and the type of books they are publishing. The two of us had spent long hours discussing which of many we believed would be most receptive, and we had finally selected a leading New York house because of their recent success with several motivational and self-help books.

I remember so well that special morning when Louise placed the carefully wrapped typescript in my hand to bring to the post office. She kissed me and said softly, "Joshua Croydon would be very proud of how you've used his old typewriter."

V

MY ELATION AND PRIDE AT HAVING COMPLETED THE BOOK were soon displaced by a terrible feeling of emptiness, much worse than the withdrawal pangs I had suffered after resigning from Treasury Insurance. We are truly all creatures of habit, and working on *A Better Way to Live* had become such a vital part of my daily routine that I was at a loss as to how to fill my days while waiting for the verdict from an editorial office on Fifth Avenue.

I was in the lighthouse, trying to keep my mind occupied by hanging scores of family pictures around the fireplace, when Louise jarred me back to reality one morning. "Okay, fella," she announced, "put your hammer away. We've got some pressing duties that just can't wait any longer."

"I'm ready. Anything! Anything! What would you like?"

"Well . . . a Christmas tree for openers."

"Oh my God! I've been so wrapped up in the book that . . ."

She took my hand and led me to the couch. As we sat facing each other she reached into her apron pocket, removed folded sheets of notebook paper and handed them to me.

"What are these?"

"Those, my love, are your sons' 'want lists.' In case the long months of writing have dulled your memory, each year at our encouragement they supply us with a rundown of specific items they'd like to receive for Christmas, and we decide, from those lists, what to buy each of them."

"I'm ready when you are. Where are we shopping?"

"You had better look at the lists," she said hoarsely.

The first sheet I unfolded was headed "Glenn," and beneath his name there was only one item printed, *album, Bee Gees, Saturday Night Fever.* On the second sheet, beneath Todd's name, there was also just one request, *a new baseball glove.*

I shook my head. "I don't get it. Those two have always managed to come up with a couple of dozen things they'd love to have, and even though they never got all their wishes, it made it a lot easier for us."

Louise was staring down at her hands.

"Louise?"

I had to lean forward to hear her. "I guess the kids realize that one gift for each is about all we can afford this year."

She was struggling to hold back the tears, and now she gripped both my hands tightly. "I cut their allowance months ago," she continued, "and began packing lunches for them instead of giving them lunch money. Also, I stopped being a soft touch."

I groaned, suddenly feeling very stupid, inconsiderate, and helpless. "Why didn't you tell me, hon? I knew we were getting low on funds, but I was so wrapped up in the book that I just kept putting it out of my mind."

"That's why I held off telling you, Mark. I didn't want to worry you while you were writing. You had enough on your mind. And don't forget, I've been the only treasurer this family has had since day one. Remember those early years when we would huddle over the kitchen table and decide what bills had to be paid and which ones could wait until your next paycheck? Then, as you kept getting promoted and your income increased, we had fewer and fewer meetings, and finally, they weren't necessary anymore. For years now I've just paid all the bills as they came due, and that left you free to concentrate on your job. That's a tough habit to break, and I'm a proud lady."

I sighed. "Okay, treasurer, you've carried the load long enough. Let me have it."

"We've got a little more than four thousand dollars in our savings and checking accounts. That will just about take care of our monthly mortgage, our utilities, and buy us food for three months if we skimp."

"But what about Christmas? Gifts?"

She buried her face on my shoulder. "I don't know, hon. We just can't afford . . ."

I stroked her hair, trying to think of the right words. "Louise, I wouldn't trade the last two years for a mountain of gold. We've done everything we said we would do . . . and the book was written. Now we've got to have faith, the same kind of faith that has helped us to handle every problem we've ever had and win. Listen to me. You and I are going out shopping for the kids just as we always did. Do you have any idea what they want besides a damn record album and a baseball glove?"

"They need clothes, Mark. Desperately. You know how boys go through shirts and pants and shoes, and I haven't bought them anything for I can't remember how long. They're starting to look like a couple of neglected orphans."

"Okay, let's get into gear and go shopping like we always have."

"No, Mark," she cried, shaking her head. "Not like always! We can't."

"All right, we'll set a limit. A hundred dollars on each kid, and you and I solemnly swear to spend no more than fifty dollars on each other. Deal?"

"Deal," she said, smiling wanly.

"With one condition."

"Huh?"

"You're still doing all the wrapping."

We declared the lighthouse off limits to our sons and it became the repository for the gifts that Louise and I bought in the next two weeks. We shopped in Keene and Peterborough and one day even ventured down to Boston to search for bargains in the basement of our favorite department store, Jordan Marsh. The jostling crowds, the piped-in Christmas carols, the laughter, the shining faces of little children, the church choirs in various malls, all of these were the perfect medicine to cure our blues. I loved every moment except for the painful decisions Louise and I had to make, usually in noisy crowded restaurants, as we struggled to balance our limited purchases equally between the two boys.

On the Saturday before Christmas, at his request, I drove Todd to see Santa Claus at the Sears store in Keene. I'll never forget that look of wonder and awe on his small face as he sat stiffly on Santa's knee and haltingly repeated that he had been a good boy all year. But even more memorable was the aftermath. As we were leaving the store he suddenly let go of my hand and raced up to a counter displaying the largest stuffed teddy bear I had ever seen.

"Daddy," he yelled as he pointed, "can I give Mom that for Christmas?"

"A teddy bear for Mom?"

"Please, Daddy, please. Mom told me that when she was a little girl she had a teddy bear, but his arm broke off and he died. She cried a lot, she said. Now she can have a new friend to play with. Please! I'll pay you when we get home. I have money in my piggy bank."

I had only twelve dollars in my wallet. Quick decision. Going against my treasurer's stern edict, I charged the huge animal on my MasterCard, and somehow we managed to smuggle Teddy, wrapped in a giant plastic bag, into the barn without Louise seeing us.

Immediately after dinner, on Christmas Eve, Louise excused herself and with two shopping bags filled with wrapping paper and ribbon she headed for the lighthouse for her annual ritual with the packages.

Both boys had hung their stockings on the fireplace in the living room, earlier in the day, and although Glenn had long since lost that precious innocence of believing in Saint Nick, he wasn't about to do anything to cloud his young brother's faith. After they had gone up to bed I went into our bedroom, removed my gifts for Louise from behind the clothes in my closet, and struggled helplessly at the simple task, for most, of wrapping packages. Messed it up, as always. Carrying her presents I walked softly down the hall and looked in on Glenn. The bed was empty! Then I remembered the custom they had initiated when Todd had been only three. On Christmas Eve they slept together, in Todd's bed.

I continued down the hall to Todd's room, pushed open the door, and stepped inside. Before long I could see their two faces in the soft glow from the night light in the hall. Just faintly, from the kitchen radio below, I could hear Christmas carols. Suddenly, and without even realizing what I was doing, I had fallen to my knees. Silently I began to repeat the Lord's Prayer, and as I prayed I thought of another tiny boy who slept on this night, for the first time, nearly two thousand years ago. He was not as warm as my boys, his bed was not as comfortable, and his poor father and mother were frightened and alone in a strange village.

Yet I realized, as I gazed at my two sons, that I wouldn't be on my knees, on this special night, and thinking such warm thoughts of love and gratitude for all my blessings if it had not been for that other small boy . . . and I couldn't help but wonder what his dad was thinking as he looked down on his sleeping face. Finally, I leaned across the bed and gently kissed Todd and Glenn. Then I went downstairs, placed the smaller of the two packages for Louise under the tree, and carried the other one out into the yard. A light snow was falling as I walked to the lighthouse.

Louise was exactly where I expected to find her—in the middle of the floor surrounded by wrapping paper of every color and dimension, busily cutting ribbons and expertly making bows for the stack of presents all wrapped so beautifully.

"Is it safe to come in?"

"Come ahead, Santa, your presents, such as they are, have been wrapped. And while you're standing, would you mind putting another log on the fire?"

I did as I was told and then slid down beside her. "The boys are sound asleep."

"Good. I'm almost finished," she said proudly.

"That's a change. Usually you're still at it until three or four in the morning."

She grinned. "With a two-hundred-dollar limit, this year the packages requiring my artistic talents seem to have decreased considerably in number."

"Merry Christmas," I said, handing her the present I had brought from the house. She slid over until she was on my lap before carefully removing the green wrapping paper.

"A book?" She riffled the pages. They were all pure white. "A blank book?"

"Not quite. You'll find an inscription on the first page."

She turned back the leather cover and read the words silently. Then she spoke them aloud. "To my beloved lady. Although this book may have no text, I promise that the next one I autograph to you will be filled with my very best work as well as my love. Mark."

She placed both hands on my shoulders and leaned back. "Thank you, dear. I love you very much, and I'm proud to be your wife. And don't worry about letting us down. That will never happen. You know, Mark, while I was sitting here alone, surrounded by all your books, I suddenly thought of a great name for this wonderful light-house of ours."

"A name?"

"Sure. Why not? If Irving Wallace or William Buckley owned this unique building, you can bet they'd have a large brass nameplate hanging over that outside door."

"I see. And although I haven't sold a single word for publication yet, you are already associating me with Wallace and Buckley?"

She pushed me backwards and leaped to her feet. "Do you want to hear the name or don't you?"

"Shoot!"

Louise went over to the bookshelves containing my first edition success books and ran her fingers across the bindings. Then she raised both hands high above her head, pointing to the rows of books above and shouted, "Henceforth, Mr. Christopher, this lighthouse shall be known as the Tower of Success! And within these lovely walls, already packed with knowledge and wisdom, you will continue to create sentences and paragraphs so powerful that they will become guiding beacons of light and inspiration to the entire world. I promise you!"

She removed a bottle of Chablis from the small refrigerator, and we drank a toast. The lighthouse was officially christened. "I only hope," I sighed as we touched glasses, "that I'm one tenth as successful as my predecessor here. You know, sometimes when the wind blows and that circular stairway creaks, I swear that it sounds as if Joshua Croydon were coming down those steps to reclaim his lighthouse."

"That reminds me," she said. "Don't move!"

Louise ran over to the old desk and returned with a package wrapped in gold foil. "Merry Christmas, author!"

I hefted the package for several minutes before tearing away the paper. Another book. Not one with blank pages, but an old, much-handled copy of *Bartlett's Familiar Quotations*. Louise was watching my face intently as I opened the volume to its inside cover and gasped. Scrawled in green ink was the inscription, *Joshua Croydon, 1947.*

"Where did you get this?"

"Found it in that old desk, the second day we were here. Mrs. Croydon left you the desk and typewriter, and so I'm sure she knew that book was in one of the drawers and wanted you to have it. I've had it hidden in my dresser for almost two years now. Thought it would make a very special gift on that first Christmas after you finished your book."

"What a treasure," I said, stroking the faded jacket.

"That's not all. See that bookmark? It was in the book when I found it, right where it is now. Open it to that page."

The page was 926. Circled, in the same green ink as the inscription up front, was a four-line quotation from a poem by James Elroy Flecker, a British poet of the early part of this century as I learned later.

Louise removed the volume from my hands. Her voice was little more than a whisper. "Would you like to hear the words that Mr. Croydon circled here?"

I nodded.

"Okay, close your eyes."

I did. Then I waited, for several minutes it seemed.

"Are you ready?" she called, her voice now echoing through the lighthouse. I opened my eyes. Louise was leaning over the stairway railing, halfway up the tower!

"Why are you up there?" I yelled.

"Just close your eyes and listen and you'll know why!"

I closed my eyes and listened . . .

> "Since I can never see your face,
> And never shake you by the hand,
> I send my soul through time and space
> To greet you. You will understand."

40

VI

LOUISE AND THE BOYS ARE ASLEEP. I AM HERE IN THE lighthouse, staring at these typewriter keys as I have done most of this day. The events that happened next were so filled with heartache and frustration that they are painful to recall, much less put down on paper, and yet I must. Time is running out.

Although our mailbox is at the bottom of our hill, Mr. Slattery drove his mail truck up the snow-packed driveway one morning, late in February, to deliver a bulky manila envelope on which he regretfully informed me that there was four dollars and sixty-four cents postage due.

I paid him, carried the tattered package into the kitchen, and tore it open as Louise watched silently. The publisher's form letter was brief. They were grateful for having been given the opportunity to consider my book but regretted that it did not fit in with their current editorial needs.

The passing of time usually dulls the memories of our saddest moments, but I can still vividly recall that horrible pain in the pit of my stomach when I was suddenly confronted with the numbing fact that *A Better Way to Live* had been rejected.

Louise joined me at the kitchen table but brushed aside the rejection note without reading it. She was more concerned with the sorry condition of the typescript that she had prepared with so much care.

"Mark, look at these pages. Nearly every one is wrinkled or folded."

"I guess that's our fault, hon. We forgot to enclose some kind of a heavy padded envelope, self-addressed with postage, for its safe return. We probably should be grateful that they bothered to send it back at all."

"No problem. I'll type it again. We've got two carbon copies, but I read somewhere that editors prefer reading the original. And don't look so forlorn. This is just God's way of testing us. One rejection doesn't mean anything. Did you know that *Jonathan Livingston Seagull* was rejected twenty times before it was published?"

Just five days later I brought a freshly typed copy of the book to the post office and mailed it to the next publisher on a list we had compiled. This time we included a self-addressed heavy envelope with return postage, and after dinner that evening, I announced that I had a new job and was starting in the morning, early.

"Where, Dad?" Todd and Glenn asked in unison.

"I'm going to work in the sawmill."

"Doing what?"

"I'll be part of a crew running those big pine logs through the saws, cutting them up into rough boards."

"Mark, you're not!" Louise cried, her face almost colorless.

"Yes, I am. I've had my application in since before Christmas, and when I stopped by today, after mailing the book, they hired me. I did exactly the same work in a mill outside of Bangor for almost a year after high school. I'll be okay."

"But that was more than twenty years ago! You're not in shape for that kind of hard labor. And isn't it dangerous?"

"The first couple of weeks will be tough, but I can take it. And no, it's not dangerous . . . if everyone is careful. They haven't had an accident at this mill in years."

"Mark—"

"Louise, at least this will give us grocery money, and it will be good for me. I'll be out in the fresh air all day, and when we sell the book I'll quit. Fair enough?"

I was ready to quit after the first few hours. Wrestling huge logs, most of them twelve feet long and more than two feet in diameter, was sheer torture. My muscles didn't ache, they burned, while my feet nearly froze. It's cold in Jaffrey in March, especially at seven in the morning when our workday began. Of course, the early starting hour meant that I was home by three-thirty or so every afternoon. That still gave me some time with the boys, except that they usually returned from school to find me sleeping on the living room couch until Louise revived me for dinner.

A Better Way to Live was returned to us again in late April. Just as distressing was a letter from our bank informing us that we were now a month in arrears on our mortgage payments. After a long and painful discussion, which included two tearful boys, we placed a classified ad in our weekly paper and sold our Jeep Wagoneer, the magic carpet that had transported us to so many happy times. We bought an old Chevrolet pickup truck with part of the proceeds.

When the book was rejected for the third time, Louise made her gallant move to save the sinking ship. She drove the pickup to Keene and got a job. As a waitress. From five to midnight, six nights a week. Together we were now earning in a month less than my weekly salary had been with Treasury Insurance. Not exactly what I had in mind when I had said farewell to Mr. Hadley in his library, three years earlier. Three years! Had it been that long since I had boldly told him that I felt I was better able to cope with rainy days than most?

The fourth publisher on our list returned the typescript in September, again with only a form letter. None of the four, apparently, thought that the book even merited any personal constructive criticism from any editor, and so I decided to solicit some. I mailed a carbon copy of *A Better Way to Live* to my old friend, Adrian Crawshaw, the antiquarian book dealer on Boston's Beacon Street from whom I had purchased all my cherished first editions. My attached letter was brief. For old time's sake would he please take the time to read what I had written and give me his opinion, with no punches pulled. He responded swiftly, in his precise script, stating that he believed the book had considerable merit, was eminently readable, and certainly of a quality not found very often lately among the glut of printed trash (his words) pretending to be self-help books. He also very diplomatically reminded me that he was certain he could find buyers for some of the first editions he had sold me over the years.

Early in January, when the towering piles of rough lumber had filled the storage yard to capacity, the sawmill was shut down for an indefinite period, which we were told would be at least three months. Driving home, with my last paycheck in my wallet and a lump in my throat, I stopped at Mac's Blue Sunoco station for gas. After a long wait at the pumps, I finally jumped from the truck and was pumping my own when Mac appeared, out of breath.

"Sorry, Mr. Christopher."

"Where's all your help?"

"Are you kidding? Who wants to work in a filling station these days?"

"I do."

Mac was a magician with a wrench or a screwdriver, and we arranged our duties accordingly. He did all the repairs and tune-ups while I manned the pumps, changed flats, and handled whatever road service jobs we got. I was in my new "position" less than a week when I ran out to wait on a green Cadillac Eldorado, early one morning, and immediately wished that the ground would open up and swallow me. Bob Boynton, Treasury's branch manager in Keene, who had discovered the Croydon property for us, was staring at me openmouthed from behind the wheel.

"Mark, is that you?"

"Hi, Bob, how's it going?"

"What are you doing here? How come you're not up on the hill, banging away at your typewriter?"

What could I say? I remember mumbling something about the first book being finished and we were waiting to hear from the publisher.

"Great! So what's this all about?" he asked, nodding at my uniform.

"Oh, just helping out a friend. Mac got a little short-handed and—"

"I heard you were working at the mill, Mark."

I nodded. There aren't many secrets in rural New Hampshire. "Just until I sell the book, Bob. You know how kids are. They like to eat, at least three times a day."

He forced a grin and nodded. "We miss you, Mark. All of us. Including Mr. Hadley."

"How is the old boy?"

"Just great. Sends you his best. We were all in Boston for a sales conference last week. Wasn't the same without you."

Bob began fiddling with his steering wheel. I moved close to his window and leaned in. "Come on, old buddy, we've known each other too long to play games. What's on your mind?"

"Well . . . ," he hesitated. "Doggone, Mark, Hadley heard that things were not going too well for you, and he asked me to tell you that if you're of a mind, you might want to give him a call someday. We've had two hot shots go down for the count trying to handle this New England region . . ."

"You could handle it, Bob."

"No way. I'm too old to be jumping around six states coddling seven hundred salespeople, and after the great job you did anyone would be a fool to try to follow that class act. Nope. I'll just stay in Keene and make my fifty grand the easy way. After twenty-five years at it I guess I'm just getting lazy. The motivation ain't there anymore, Mark, you know what I mean."

I patted his shoulder, and he drove away. Never even bought gas.

Louise found me that evening, in the lighthouse, packing my first editions into several cartons.

"What are you doing, Mark?"

"I'm going to take some of these old dust collectors down to Boston, tomorrow, and see if Mr. Crawshaw can convert them into dollars for us."

"Darling, you can't! Those books mean so much to you."

I tucked an Alger edition gently into the carton

before reaching out and taking her hands. "Isn't the mortgage overdue again?"

She sighed and nodded.

"Bob Boynton was in the station this morning. I guess that Hadley knows about our—our plight. He'd like me to give him a phone call. Shall I? Shall I phone him, hon?"

Her brown eyes glistened, and she replied immediately. "Sell the books, Mark! We can replace them. We're not raising the white flag, not now, not ever! We'll make it. Just remember *Jonathan Livingston Seagull*."

Mr. Crawshaw purchased nine of my first editions and wrote me out a check for seventeen hundred dollars. As desperately as we needed the money, I was almost relieved that he didn't take all of them. Still, it was a long ride back to Jaffrey. Parting with those precious volumes was like selling off part of my family.

In March we shifted our tactics. Since we had not been able to get so much as a nibble out of any of the major publishers, Louise suggested that we approach one of the smaller ones and she had circled three names in *Writer's Market*. One of them caught my eye. "I know that one. Charles Bergen Publishers. They've published some excellent books on psychology and salesmanship and success. Quality material and reputable authors. I see that this Bergen is not just the publisher, he is also the only editor listed. Probably runs a shoestring operation, but something tells me that he's our guy."

And so, accompanied by the usual brief letter that did little more than synopsize my career and credentials in a single paragraph, the typescript of *A Better Way to Live* was mailed to Charles Bergen Publishers.

Our fortune was about to change. Luckily for us, we didn't know it.

VII

ON A WARM AFTERNOON IN MAY I WAS RUNNING AN ancient cultivator through our garden, preparing the stubborn moist soil for spring planting, when Louise's shouts broke in on the noisy and hypnotic putt-putt of the small three-horsepower engine. She was waving frantically from the back porch, a behavior very unlike her, and so I raced toward the house without even pausing to shut off the motor.

"Telephone," was all she said, looking as if she had just won the grand prize in the New Hampshire Lottery.

I started inside, but she tugged on my jacket just as I opened the door, and when I turned she kissed me. "It's Charles Bergen, Mark!"

The voice on the phone sounded hoarse and ancient, and I had visions of an elderly gentleman sitting at a rolltop desk wearing a plastic green eyeshade and fancy arm garters.

"Mr. Christopher, you have written an absolutely marvelous book. I would very much like to publish it."

"Sir, that's great news! I would very much like to have you publish it!"

"I understand, from your letter, that you were an insurance executive for many years. Tell me, did you do much writing in that position?"

"Not really. I've given many speeches, usually the motivational kind, to my salespeople, and I did make some pretty thorough notes for those, but that's about as close as I've come to writing anything."

"Amazing. You have great talent. You make your points with clarity and eloquence, and there is also a spiritual quality in your style, sometimes even poetic, that reminds me of Marcus Bach or Loren Eiseley."

"I'm familiar with the writings of both, Mr. Bergen, and I can't think of a greater compliment."

"Mr. Christopher, we are a small publishing house, but we are very proud of the fine books and authors we have published over the years. As a matter of fact, one of our talented authors lived up your way. Perhaps you knew him?"

"Who sir?"

"Joshua Croydon, the naturalist."

"Mr. Bergen, I'm living in his house and writing in his studio; however, I never had the honor of meeting the man. He passed away, as you perhaps know, three years ago. We purchased this place from his widow."

"I can remember my father talking about Mr. Croydon's unique inland lighthouse that was also his studio. Dad visited the Croydons once, and we still have a picture, hanging here in my office, of Mr. Croydon with his arm around my father, standing outside the lighthouse. Dad founded this publishing company more than forty years ago, and he ran it until he died in 1975. His name was Charles, as is mine, so we remain as before, Charles Bergen Publishing."

"I see."

"Mr. Christopher, we are prepared to pay you an advance of three thousand dollars for your fine book. If your book does well, and I truly believe it has great potential, you will be well rewarded in the future through your royalty checks which are payable to you twice a year. I'll send you two copies of our standard contract. Have your attorney look them over, and if the terms are acceptable, we'll get into action. Although it's already May, I believe that if we hurry we can still get your book on our fall list and have it in the stores in time to take advantage of the holiday buying."

I knew that there were scores of questions I should be asking, but it was all happening too fast for me to think of anything except that I had finally sold my book. "That sounds great to me," I replied.

"I want to assure you, Mr. Christopher, that we will extend every effort within our means to bring your excellent book to the public's attention. They need your book. They need it desperately. Good self-help books have become a rarity in the past ten or fifteen years. My father was always wondering where the new Napoleon Hills and Dale Carnegies were. He would have loved your book. It is put together in the old classic style of the very best success books, has plenty of good practical information that anyone can use to change his or her life for the better and, most important, it is easy to read. I really believe you have a winner, Mr. Christopher!"

"Mr. Bergen, I hope you're right. I've got a lot riding on that book."

There was a long pause. "You are not presently employed?"

"Part time. In a filling station. I resigned from my company almost four years ago and moved up here from Massachusetts with my wife and two sons, to write."

I heard a subdued chuckle. "I see that you follow your own advice, Mr. Christopher."

"How's that?"

"In one of your chapters you deal with the advantage, even the necessity on some occasions, of burning one's bridges behind. You go on to explain, as I recall, that when one's avenue of retreat is cut off there is only one way to go—forward. I would like to inquire about one other matter before we part, Mr. Christopher. I was wondering how many publishers did you submit your book to before you got around to sending it to me?"

I hesitated. Did I dare tell him that four of the largest had turned thumbs down on my work? How would he take it?

"Four," I said, and named them.

I heard something that sounded like a chuckle. "Well," he said, "I'm certainly not in their league. What made you choose me?"

"My wife had narrowed the field down to three small publishers, and yours was the only name I knew, especially your reputation for publishing quality. That's all there was to it."

"Amazing. And to think that you wrote this fine book in Joshua Croydon's old studio. I believe it was Shakespeare who wrote, 'Heaven from all creatures hides the book of fate.' We will do our very best not to keep your book hidden, that I promise you. Have a good day, sir."

Late in July I completed checking the publisher's

proofs for punctuation and typographical errors, with Louise's invaluable help. We were in our kitchen, with elongated galley sheets spread across the entire table, when we finally finished the last numbered page. Louise capped her red Flair pen and sighed. "Have you noticed, Mark, how much more important the words seem now that they are set in type? They're still you, but now they have a distinctive ring of authority to them. I'm beginning to understand for the first time how powerful an influence any book can be, for bad or good. One's mind almost automatically assumes that whatever is being read from a book must be true, and I know I've often felt that way even when reading fiction. It's a little scary, isn't it? Well, we're finished. Now what?"

"We pack these up and return them to Bergen. Then we wait for our grand debut into the publishing world, which Charles said would be October seventh."

A few weeks later Charles Bergen called. "Mr. Christopher, in our haste to put your book together we forgot one item. It's an old custom but most authors still like to do it. Is there anyone in particular to whom you'd like to dedicate your book? That page will appear following the title page. If you do have someone in mind could you possibly give me the wording over the phone, now?"

"I'll call you back in twenty minutes, Mr. Bergen. Okay?"

"Very well."

I called him back in less than ten and read him the words I had just scribbled on the back of an envelope . . .

"To that beautiful redhead whom I have missed for many, many years—my mother, Margaret."

VIII

THE OCTOBER DEBUT OF *A Better Way to Live* INTO THE
seemingly infinite world of more than 20,000 new fall
books attracted about as much attention as a lonely baseball fan making his way into the crowded bleachers at
Yankee Stadium on a Sunday afternoon.

No one noticed. A clipping service that Charles
Bergen subscribed to could not find a single review, either
positive or negative, in any newspaper in the country
during those first few weeks after publication, despite his
assurance that more than four hundred copies had been
sent to book review editors.

Now I could relate to that terrible feeling of helplessness that I had heard so many authors describe on talk
shows. A new book is very much like a child. Sooner or
later it must go out into the world and succeed or fail on
its own, usually leaving behind one or two loving people
filled with concern and guilt and wondering if they had

truly done all they could have to prepare their issue for the cruel marketplace of life.

Holding a copy of my book for the first time, with its well-designed scarlet jacket accenting the gold block letters of the title, was a thrill. Even greater was our elation at discovering copies for sale at The Apple Tree bookstore in Concord, sharing important front table display space with the latest nonfiction efforts of Tom Wolfe, Henry Kissinger, and Edmund Morris. I almost had to restrain Louise physically to prevent her from blurting out, to every store clerk and customer, that the man she was with, *her husband*, had written that book with the lovely red and gold jacket. And although we had twenty-five copies at home that we had just received from Charles, Louise insisted on buying one for good luck.

Still, a nagging fear of failure refused to fade from my mind despite all my past experiences on how to deal with that monster. What if the book was a dud? What about distribution? Was the book on sale in stores across the country? Charles Bergen had no book representatives of his own, as did the major publishers, salespeople who called regularly on stores and chains to push their products. Instead, he shared a group of independent commissioned agents with five other small publishers. What kind of a job had they done with my book? Also, how much influence did they have on a bookstore buyer compared with a representative from Doubleday or Harper & Row?

And then a miracle happened. Two days before Thanksgiving, Charles Bergen phoned, sounding as low-keyed as always.

"Mr. Christopher, I have some news that will make 'our holiday turkey taste twice as delicious!"

"I can use some, sir."

"If you are not sitting down, I suggest that you do so."

I sat.

"Mr. Christopher, the first printing of your book, as I'm sure I told you, was ten thousand copies. Usually on a first printing, by any unknown author, I would print no more than five thousand, but I had great faith in this one so I doubled up. Well, my friend, that entire first printing is already sold out, and we have just gone back to press for twenty thousand more copies! The leading chains, Dalton and Waldenbooks, have each just ordered three thousand copies! Those are the two largest orders we have received in our history. Their hundreds of stores are all on computer, and I understand that there isn't a single copy of your book unsold in any of the outlets that stocked it. I think we're on to something very big here."

"Wow! How do you explain it? After all, there has been no publicity or promotion. Not even a book review anywere. What's triggering those sales, Mr. Bergen?"

"There's no logical explanation, Mark. By the way, may I call you Mark after all this time? And please, call me Charles . . . but not Charley. I believe that what we are experiencing here is that mysterious process which confounds all advertising experts. Good old 'word of mouth.' Every now and then a book or movie or a song appears with no hype or hullabaloo, but the public still discovers it, and a love affair begins. Happens every five or ten years in the publishing business, and when it does the results can be mind boggling. *Games People Play*, by Berne, was the last book I can remember that rode that beautiful wave. If this keeps up, the sky's the limit."

"Are you getting re-orders from all parts of the country, or are we—"

"From everywhere!" he interrupted. "And many of the stores are not even bothering to contact our reps. They're calling me direct! Never happened before. I've sold almost two thousand copies on the phone this morning. Stores in Tacoma, Butte, Kansas City, both of them, Memphis. Ward's Corner Book Shop in Norfolk, Va. just gave me an order for five hundred copies before I phoned you! Amazing. I've never seen anything like this, and I don't believe my father ever did either. If the orders keep coming in I may have to go right back to press for a third printing. I've already hired two more people for our shipping department just to keep ahead of the orders."

He phoned again, two weeks later, this time not sounding so low-keyed.

"Mark, we've just gone back to press again. This time for forty thousand more, and almost eighteen thousand of those are to fill orders! Every day we're getting calls from stores we have never done business with before, and I've hired three more people to help with the billing and shipping. I can't believe this! I can't!"

"Charles, do you have any profile by now? Who's buying all those books? Have we touched a nerve with a certain group, or is it too early for you to get a fix on that?"

"I've already had the reps checking on this, and the bookstores report that everyone is buying it from all walks of life. Gifts. Gifts are a big thing. People apparently buy a copy for themselves, they read it, then they return to buy three more. For their kids. Their boss. Someone they love. Sales managers are buying them by the dozen for their salespeople. And women. Women, they tell me, are accounting for more than half the sales. You've touched them all. Mark. It's a miracle . . . it truly is!"

Three weeks later he phoned to tell me that his

fourth printing was an astonishing one hundred thousand copies. Astonishing since ninety-five percent of all books published never even reach the ten thousand mark in sales. Charles repeated that press run, ten days later, and now the total copies in print had reached the staggering figure of two hundred and seventy thousand! By my nervous computations, if all those copies were sold, they would earn me more than three hundred thousand dollars in royalties. Scratch one waitress and one filling station attendant.

Newsweek finally reviewed the book, calling it a milestone in the self-help field, comparable to *Think and Grow Rich, How to Win Friends and Influence People* and *The Power of Positive Thinking*. By the end of May, a million hardcover copies of *A Better Way to Live* were in print; it was on the top of every bestseller list in the nation, and I was close to becoming a millionaire! A miracle indeed!

The phone calls from Charles soon became a daily ritual. Each morning, promptly at ten, he was on the line sounding like a smug stockbroker reporting to a client that his stock had just gone up another ten points. I was even informed when the plant that printed his books, in Jersey City, went on a second shift in order to keep up with his print orders, and they were beginning to encounter problems finding enough paper to handle the massive printings.

Then he phoned, one morning, with what he thought were two major problems.

"Mark, you just cannot remain in hiding in that lighthouse of yours any longer. The media people are driving me crazy. Someone from the *Today Show* has called every morning this week; I just hung up after talking to a production assistant at *Good Morning, America,* and now Johnny Carson's people are pushing, and they never chase anybody. They don't have to."

"What are you telling all of them?"

"Just what you told me. That you don't do interviews. That your book speaks for you and that should be enough. Are you sure you won't change your mind? That kind of national publicity we can't buy, at any price."

"My God, Charles, you won't be satisfied until you have that printing plant working twenty-four hours a day."

"Why not? It's a once-in-a-lifetime shot."

"No interviews, Charles. I've seen too many authors make asses of themselves on talk shows. Put me on one of those big television shows, and I'm liable to put my foot in my mouth and bring the sales of our book to a screaming halt. And I don't want to have to answer all those dumb questions, over and over, on what I eat for breakfast or what my hobbies are or whether or not I sleep in the nude. For most authors I guess all that is a great ego trip, but most of them are already so puffed up with their imagined importance that they have no idea how silly they sound."

"You really mean that don't you, Mark? Okay, how about reporters? Listen, I've got a list of requests for interviews here that you would not believe. Any other author in the world would kill for the chance to talk with this gang . . . *The Wall Street Journal, The New York Times, Psychology Today, The Washington Post, The San Francisco Chronicle,* even *The National Enquirer—*"

"What, no *People* magazine?"

"You want *People,* I'll get *People!* Give me thirty minutes—"

"Charles, I'm only kidding. I don't want any of them. I'm too busy planting my garden and helping coach my youngest kid's Little League team, and there's still a lot of this part of the world that we haven't seen yet."

"And what about your mail?"

"What mail?"

"Your fan mail, Mark, your fan mail! It's pouring in here from all over the country. Canada too. What should we do with it?"

"Forward the letters to me, and I'll answer them. How's that?"

"All of them?"

"Of course."

"That you will do, but no interviews?"

"There's a big difference, Charles. If someone out there was influenced enough by the book to take the time to write, they deserve a reply."

"But if you answer your mail, won't everyone know where you are?"

"Not necessarily. I'll write on plain stationery and mail the letters in Concord. No return address."

He hung up in utter frustration.

On another morning I was out shopping and missed his call. Louise was sitting at the kitchen table when I returned, and I could tell as soon as I saw the look on her face that she was about to lay something heavy on me. I dropped the two grocery bags on the counter and slid a chair up close to her.

"Okay, let me have it before you bust."

"*Time* wants to do a cover story on you!"

I started to rise, but she reached over and pushed me back down on the chair gently. "Hold on, Mark. You really should consider this. Poor Charles was almost in tears. He begged me to try to convince you. They want to send two reporters and a photographer, and they'd like to do it as soon as possible. Very few authors get a shot at that spot. Why don't you do it?"

I poured myself a cup of coffee before answering.

"You know why I won't, Louise. We went over all this just a couple of weeks ago, and nothing has changed. If we start playing the media game, our life will become a circus and this place will turn into a zoo."

She reached across the table and stroked the back of my hand. "Now calm down and listen. Think about the hell we've gone through in the past year or so. Neither you nor I, in our wildest dreams, ever came close to imagining that all this would be happening to us. Knowing you, if you had seen it coming, you probably never would have written the book. But—it has happened and I'm not certain, yet, that you realize what you've done. Charles told me that if sales continue as they are going, you are certain to become the bestselling self-help author of all time, even bigger than Peale or Carnegie or anyone else. And those nice people out there, who must be getting so much from your book, deserve to know the man behind it. Forget the money and the fame and all the other so-called benefits you would receive from all that exposure on television and in the press, and think, instead, of the thousands who are reaching out to you. You can't turn your back on them because it doesn't happen to fit in with your lifestyle. You can't! If you really believe in that book, and I know you do, then you've got to come out of your tower and let the world see you, know you . . . and love you. You've got to . . ."

The front door chimes saved me, or so I thought. Mr. Slattery, our mailman, was standing on the porch, hat in hand, scratching his bald head and grinning. In the driveway was a large mail truck instead of his usual jeep.

"Mr. Christopher, I've got some mail for you, and it just wouldn't fit in the mail box."

"Okay, let's have it, Tom."

"Where do you want it, sir? I've got eighteen bags out in the truck. We figure that you must have at least six thousand letters. Ain't never seen anything like it before. Should keep you busy for a while," he chuckled.

Long after Mr. Slattery had helped me carry the mail bags into the lighthouse, Louise and I, still in shock, stood staring at the large pile of canvas containers in silence. Finally, she reached down, untied the knot on one of the bags, placed her hand inside, and removed a single pink envelope. She tore it open carefully, removed a sheet of lined paper, unfolded it, and ran her eyes down the page.

Then, she looked my way, to make certain I was paying attention, cleared her throat, and read: "Dear Mr. Christopher . . . You have saved my life. Recently, I went through a terrible divorce and lost the custody of my two children to my husband. I was positive there was nothing left to live for. Through my own stupidities I had failed all those who were important to me and loved me, and I was close to taking my own life when my sister, Anne, who has always been very dear to me, gave me a copy of your book. It lay on my night table for at least a week, unread, as I cried myself to sleep night after night. And then, about a month ago, something made me pick up your book after I had crawled into bed. I read right through the dark hours. You have touched me deeply. You have made me understand that I still have much to offer the world, that I am a creation of God even with all my weaknesses, and that I'm entitled to another chance to live a better life providing that I choose to take it. You have given me that courage, dear Mr. Christopher, and I thank you with all of my heart. God bless you for lighting a candle in the darkness of my miserable soul."

Louise's eyes followed me as I paced back and forth.

Only an occasional creak from the circular stairway broke the stillness of the lighthouse.

"Okay," I finally mumbled. "Call Charles. Tell him I'll see those people from *Time*."

IX

LESS THAN AN HOUR AFTER LOUISE PHONED A JUBILANT Charles with my decision, he called back. She lifted the receiver, listened for a short time, said, "Okay," and hung up.

"The people from *Time* will be here on Friday morning, Mark. Driving up from Boston. That gives us less than four days to get organized."

"The mail?"

She nodded. "If we don't get it under control, it will bury us in a month."

After a hasty stop at our bank, to transfer some of our newly acquired royalty funds from our savings to our checking account, we headed for our favorite stationery store in Peterborough. In a buying orgy that lasted more than three hours we spent nearly four thousand dollars! The proprietors were so elated that they loaded all our purchases onto their delivery truck, followed us home, and placed everything in the lighthouse exactly where Louise directed.

"There you are, sir," Louise crowed triumphantly after they had gone. "Now we're in business!"

"I'm still a little confused, lady. Maybe now you'll explain to me why we need two extra desks and two more typewriters?"

"So that we can get your mail out. I'll work at one of these desks, and Mary Mellon will be at the other. Together we'll be able to—"

"Hold it . . . hold it! Who is Mary Mellon?"

"Mark, you're so terrible at remembering names. You've met Mary. She lives in town, next to the firehouse, with her crippled father. She was a school teacher in Rindge. I know she can type, and I'm positive she can use the money."

"I don't get it. I always thought the girl I married had ethics and scruples. You and Mary can't answer my mail. Wouldn't be right."

She tossed me her patented look of exasperation and stormed to the far corner of the lighthouse, returning with four large brown envelopes. "Mark, there's nothing dishonest in our helping you. Do you suppose that Michener and Herriot personally answer every letter they receive? Yesterday morning, while you were at the ballgame with Todd, I came out here and selected, at random, one hundred letters from the mail bags. I figured they would be a good test sample of what we would find among all the letters."

"And what did you find, Mrs. Gallup?"

"Your mail seems to break down into four categories. More than half of them, fifty-five out of the hundred, are from people just writing to thank you for having written *A Better Way to Live*. You would probably answer all of them with just a simple line or two, acknowledging their kind words, am I correct?"

"That would be about it."

"So, once you answer any letter which falls into category one and give Mary and me a copy of your reply, we can type a similar response to every other letter of that sort, and all you'll have to do is sign them. Okay?"

I couldn't keep from smiling at her intensity. "Okay."

"Now, thirty-four of the hundred sample letters I read contain a request for an autographed picture of you."

"That explains why you bought two thousand special photograph mailing envelopes. But I don't even have a decent picture to send anyone."

"No problem. We'll get that *Time* photographer, when he comes, to shoot some head and shoulder shots of you, and we'll buy them from him. Then we can select the best one and get it copied. I found a company in Concord who will make as many duplicate glossies as we need, and they're not all that expensive in volume. You can autograph them before Mary and I send them out."

"All right, that takes care of fifty-five percent of my mail which is in the first category and, let's see, thirty-four percent in category two, requesting photographs. That's eighty-nine percent of my mail. What about? . . ."

She raised both hands above her head. "Patience. Don't get ahead of me, now. The third category, and there were only eight in that hundred I read, are from people who seem sincere and are writing to ask you for specific advice. Those letters, Mark, I'm sure you'd want to answer yourself, although some of them will tear your heart open. I had no idea how many people out there are crying for help."

"People with all the potential in the world, Louise. But they've been knocked down so many times that they've lost all faith in themselves and in everything else. Then I guess, according to your random sample, that I can plan on answering eight or so letters out of every hundred we get, and that's category three. What's in that fourth envelope?"

"Strange mail, 'kook' letters. I found only three like that out of the hundred. One was a request for money, lots of it, because you must be so rich. Another writes that you may be a reincarnation of Christ because no one else could write such beautiful words filled with so much wisdom. She wants to organize a new church with your help. And the third is just plain obscene."

"No proposals of marriage? I thought celebrities always got tons of marriage offers."

"Well, there weren't any in this first sampling, but I'll bet you'll get them. Especially when they see what you look like. I'm sure you'll get plenty of other tempting offers, too."

"And you'll be screening all those, of course."

"Mary, too. A little titillation for a nice old spinster won't hurt her a bit. Seriously, Mark, what I think we'll do is set aside all strange letters along with those we think you should personally answer. You can look them over and decide how you want to handle them. The smart thing will probably be to ignore those that fall into category four."

I kissed her. "Thank you. I like your plan. Except for one thing. How can I possibly sit over there at my desk and write a second book with you two, close by, banging away on your typewriters all day?"

"I'm way ahead of you. This setup will only be temporary. As soon as we move the junk out of our big guest room, we'll transfer this operation to the house. Mary and I can work out of there, and after we sort the mail, each day, we'll bring your little pile to you to handle when you have time. You can drop in on us, late each day, to sign your other letters. You'll be back in virtual solitary, the way you like it, in a month or so."

Mary Mellon started work the next morning, and although it wasn't in our planned routine, I had to join them, at least for the first few days, in reading letters and categorizing them. A humbling experience. Letters from executives, salespeople, teachers, prisoners, housewives, cancer victims, athletic coaches, college students, and so many other classifications that as I read I realized Charles Bergen had been correct. The book had succeeded in cutting across all layers of society and managed to rekindle that flame of hope in almost every reader. Throughout that first day the three of us constantly interrupted the silent reading of the others with exclamations such as, "Listen to this!" "You won't believe this one!" and "This is the best one, so far!" And many times I looked up to see either Louise or Mary in tears.

Late in the day, Louise called out from her desk, "Mark?"

"Yes?"

"Do you know anyone named Salom?"

"Nope. I don't think so."

She rose from her desk, carried a single letter to me, and dropped it, envelope face down, on top of the one I was reading. "Look at this."

We've been married a long time. There was a strange and unfamiliar vibratto in her voice that made me glance up instantly.

"Are you all right, Louise?"

"Read that one."

I removed a card, perhaps four inches square, from the buff-colored envelope. It was bordered in gold, and the words on it were in the most delicate calligraphy I had ever seen . . .

You have reminded the world, in your excellent book, that one of man's greatest gifts from God is his power of choice.

Your choices, in recent years, have required courage and faith. Eventually, you will be called upon to use this great power once more, and the choice you must make will be the most difficult you have ever faced.

The card was signed *A. B. Salom.*

I forced a smile. "Another one for our 'kook' file, huh?"

"Mark, I removed that letter from one of those canvas mail bags, myself. Turn the envelope over and look at how it's addressed."

I flipped the envelope and saw *Mark Christopher* in the same blue-inked calligraphy. "There's no address, Louise! All the others are addressed to me in care of Charles Bergen Publishing. But there's nothing on this one except my name. How could it possibly have been delivered here?"

"Is that all you notice, Mark?" she asked, her voice now almost childish in pitch.

I stared at the envelope again. "My God, there's no stamp on the envelope! There isn't even a postmark!"

X

TRUE TO HER WORD, LOUISE MOVED OUR "MAIL DEPART-ment" out of the lighthouse and into the large guest room three weeks later with the assistance of two muscular high schoolers from the neighborhood. As a memento of her brief occupation of my hideaway she left behind a small pine-framed bulletin board hanging close to my desk. She said she planned to use it frequently to jog my memory on important forthcoming events like driving the boys to the barber shop and other missions that I was always conveniently forgetting under the guise of having my mind completely on my writing.

Although we discussed it no further, another reminder was also tacked to the corner of our bulletin board—the mysterious Mr. Salom's cryptic message in blue calligraphy.

The *Time* interview that I had dreaded turned out to be an exhilarating experience. Not only had John Christy and Donna Templeton read my book, which was evident by the perceptive questions they asked, but their easygoing manner soon put me completely at ease. Our discussion ranged far beyond my own personal background and the principles of achievement covered in *A Better Way to Live.* Although both correspondents, as *Time* classifies their hardworking field reporters, had tape recorders constantly running, they still filled page after page with notes as we explored the evolution of self-help literature in the United States.

John Christy, before we began, had apologized for the absence of their photographer. Roger Meyer had been delayed on another story, in Boston; however, he would arrive in the morning. John regretted any inconvenience that might cause me and did warn me that Roger would probably be around for two or three days, shadowing me, and would not leave until he was positive he had captured the real Mark Christopher on film.

Late in the day, over coffee, Donna Templeton stretched her long blue-jeaned legs, eyes fixed on the fireplace embers, and sighed, "I don't want this day to end. It's so calm and peaceful here, and I've learned so much today. You've given me a whole new picture of what true success is all about, Mr. Christopher, and I know I'll be better at my job, from now on, just from having been with you and listened."

John Christy stroked his perfectly trimmed gray beard and nodded. "You're a lucky man, Mark. There are few who would not envy you. You had a dream and you made it come true."

I walked over to the window and beckoned to John. "See that old beat up Chevy pickup truck? It's been our only means of transportation for more than a year."

He chuckled. "And now you and Louise can afford 'his' and 'her' Mercedes."

"That's not the point. We're going to keep that old clunker forever, even if we have to retire it to the barn. It will always be around to remind us of the tough times. Dreams and goals are wonderful things to have, but if they're worthwhile, they usually carry a stiff price tag. I emphasize that point in my book. Churchill's great phrase, 'blood, sweat, and tears' also happens to be a pretty good formula for success, but it's a tough one to sell, these days."

Donna glanced at her wristwatch and looked in John's direction. He nodded. "I think that about covers it all, Mark, but I've got one more question before we leave you. Now that you've written this great bestseller and you have all the money and security you could possibly want, what is your goal in life?"

It was an innocent and legitimate question, but for the first time, all day, I hesitated before replying. I could feel both of them staring at me, waiting, as I fiddled with my wristwatch strap. Finally, I heard myself saying, "I would like the privilege of living long enough to see both my boys become men."

Donna kissed my cheek as she was getting into their rented Oldsmobile. I was sorry to see them go.

Midway through the following morning, while I was mowing the lawn, our photographer arrived—in a growling 280Z. Roger Meyer remained as our guest over the weekend, sleeping in Glenn's room while the boys doubled up. He captivated both of them, sat on their bed at night, and told them many of his adventures with a camera. He taught them how to hold, focus, aim and shoot his Nikon and took them for a tour of Jaffrey's back roads, Grand Prix style, with Todd straddling the console and whooping it up just behind the Z's two front seats.

In between his time with my sons, Roger shot pictures of me in every conceivable pose. Cultivating the garden. Coaching third base during a Little League game. At the typewriter. Up in the tower admiring the landscape. Reading my mail. Leaning on the pickup. Chopping wood. And most of all, posed in front of our lighthouse, hands on hips, smiling, frowning, grimacing, pointing. Using his wide-angle lens, he moved me back and forth, with the tower always behind me, so that he could include the entire building in his shots. In all, by the time he had finished, he shot twenty-three rolls, thirty-six exposures to a roll. Some in color but most in black and white, including two rolls of head and shoulder shots which he presented to Louise in payment, he said, for his "room and board."

Both boys moped around for days after Roger departed.

On a Monday, late in July, Charles Bergen's familiar voice was on the phone repeating the word "Magnificent!" again and again.

"Have you seen it yet, Mark? Magnificent! Magnificent!"

"Have I seen what?"

"*Time!* The cover! The article! What a great job they did! All good things . . . and they didn't rough you up at all. I was worried. And you look so young in the pictures. Also handsome. Maybe we should put your picture on the jacket. We've just gone back to press again. Fourteenth printing. That will make a total, in print, of—are you ready—two million copies! Two million! I hope you've got a good tax man. You're going to need him. And your phone. You better have Louise get you an unlisted number fast. As soon as this magazine hits you're going to start getting phone calls from everywhere. What can I say? Congratulations!" His voice broke. "If only . . . if only my father were here to see this."

Mr. Slattery personally delivered our copy of *Time* to the door the next morning. He could not, he said, bring himself to stuff that important issue into the mailbox. The cover, as I had guessed, was one of the poses Roger had taken of me in front of the lighthouse, shot from a low angle so that I seemed to be as tall as the building behind. In heavy black print, beneath the *Time* logo, were the words, "Beacon of Hope for a Troubled World." At the bottom right of the photograph, in smaller print, they had managed to squeeze in, "An exclusive interview with Mr. Success!"

Louise was pouring orange juice for herself and Mary when I walked into the kitchen carrying the magazine. I sat and waited patiently until she had read the entire article and studied each photograph with alternate tilts of her head.

"Well?"

"I love it . . . all of it. And here's what I like the most, Mark," she said, sliding the open article over to me and pointing to its last paragraph. "They close by saying that your name seems to fit you perfectly because the word Christopher means Christ-bearer."

XI

THE FLATTERING EXPOSURE IN *Time*, AS I SHOULD HAVE expected, triggered an avalanche of requests for interviews that I could not, in fairness, decline, now that my short-lived precedent of silence had been broken. In New York a harried Charles Bergen finally decided that what we both needed was a public relations firm, not to get more publicity, he hastened to explain over my groans, but to screen, coordinate, and schedule, after checking with me, the visits by reporters to our hilltop home.

During those final five months of 1981, according to Louise's count, I was interviewed ninety-six times! It became almost impossible to walk past any magazine stand, and this was especially painful in our favorite local grocery store, without being confronted by one or more Mark Christopher faces smiling at passersby from the covers of glossy periodicals and some not so glossy. Eventually, even *Newsweek* ran a favorable feature piece without any hint of rancor at having been beaten by *Time*, even though they had been the first to recognize and review the book. And our lighthouse had been photographed and featured in so many articles that it was rapidly becoming an American landmark, Charles declared boastfully.

For the most part, I enjoyed the interviews. After the first dozen or so I became very positive and polished with my responses since I was hearing the same questions time and time again. Just as a football coach studies films of his team's games in order to spot and correct weaknesses, I mentally critiqued each interview, after it was over, and if I recalled having answered a particular question weakly, I would decide what I should have said in case that question ever came up again. It always did.

I continued to refuse all invitations to fly off to anywhere for appearances on radio or television. These rebuffs were soon countered by suggestions that we tape "on location" interviews in or around the now famous lighthouse, especially for network television. These I also rejected, gracefully I hope, although poor Charles almost had a coronary when our public relations people informed him that I had turned down Barbara Walters.

Despite all my foot dragging, however, the publicity merry-go-round would not slow down. The President opened one of his televised press conferences by quoting from *A Better Way to Live*. Frank Reynolds referred to me, on the evening news, as "Mr. Success." There was a near riot in Manila when my books cleared customs and went on sale in the many bookstores belonging to the two largest chains, Alemar's and National Bookstore. Many of the players on Clemson University's football team gave credit to *A Better Way to Live* as well as Danny Ford's coaching, for their championship season. And, early in December, Charles Bergen's printing plant, now working around the clock exclusively on my book, produced their five millionth copy!

How ironic, I thought, that I had abandoned my old way of life in order to smell the roses, and now I was spending so much time in the lighthouse giving interviews or answering my mail that the lovely tea roses nurtured for so many years by the Croydons were being decimated by grubs and beetles. Worst of all, our family excursions had not resumed now that we could afford them again. No time. Saddest words ever spoken or written.

During the height of a typical late January blizzard, Louise made her dramatic announcement. The four of us were having dinner together, something that had become a rarity once more, when she suddenly tapped her fork against her water glass and said, "Now hear this, all of you! Next Monday we are flying to Phoenix, Arizona, and we're going to spend ten days in that glorious sun just having fun. Swimming, eating, going to the movies, getting a sun tan, shopping, sight-seeing, and anything else we can think of. How's that!"

I waited until the cheers subsided enough to be heard. "Louise, that's impossible. We can't leave now. There's just too much going on."

"Look, fella, I read your book. Nothing is impossible. And all this stuff can wait. We need to be together again. It's been another difficult year for all of us, and there hasn't been much sharing, especially with the boys. We'll just pack up and go. Mary and the others will look out for things while we're gone. There's nothing that can't wait two weeks and if they need us we'll only be a phone call away."

"But we won't be able to get any decent rooms in Phoenix at this late date. The better places have probably been booked solid since—since September."

She grinned. "That's when I made our reservations. As soon as I saw your royalty check. We have two adjoining rooms reserved at the Arizona Biltmore. You can't do better than the Biltmore, they tell me."

During our flight to Phoenix, Todd and Glenn, sitting directly in front of us, alternated their time at the window seat of the giant DC-10 so that they could share, in silent awe, the unfamiliar panorama slipping past them far below. It was their first flight. At one point, Todd's puzzled face appeared above the tufted headrest. "Mom?"

Louise glanced up from her crossword puzzle book. "Yes, dear?"

"I can't see any people down there."

"That's because we're so high up, almost seven miles above the ground. Even the mountains and rivers look tiny from up here."

"Is God higher up than us?"

"Much higher."

"Then . . . how does he hear our prayers and watch over us?"

"Because, Todd, God can do anything. That's why he's God."

"Oh." The still-frowning face disappeared from view. I patted her hand. "Nice try."

Whoever had advised Louise to stay at the Arizona Biltmore was right on target. Its main building, at the end of a long winding driveway bordered by palms and flower gardens, had the ambiance and genteel character of another and less frantic era, and yet every modern amenity was available to its guests. The eighty-degree weather was also a blessed change after the sub-zero temperatures and blowing snow we had left behind.

We have so many priceless memories of those too few days in the Valley of the Sun. *We.* Such a lovely word.

We shopped at Phoenix's giant Metrocenter. We ate huge steaks cooked over mesquite at Pinnacle Peak Patio and cheered the good guys in a staged Western "shoot out" after our meal. We saw our first real cowboys. We took pictures of the Praying Monk on Camelback Mountain. We rode out into the desert on very gentle Appaloosa horses that came complete with Indian guide. We climbed Squaw Peak. We rode a stagecoach and drank cold root beer at Rawhide's Golden Belle Saloon.

One afternoon, sitting near the pool and soaking up the desert sun, Todd was very close to me as we all watched his older brother doing his clown act off the diving board. I reached over and hugged my little guy. "Are you happy?"

"Oh, yes!"

"They say that if you begin a new year feeling happy that you'll be that way all year. Do you buy that?"

He was busy wiping his head in a large towel, and so his answer was partially muffled. "I-I-I-I don't know, Dad."

"What do you mean, you don't know?"

"Dad, you're always in the lighthouse with those reporters now. It will be a happy new year if all of us can do things together again, like we are right this minute."

"Well, son, I hereby make you this solemn promise," I said in my best judicial voice, raising my right hand. "God willing, this team will have a great year in 1982, just like we did when we first moved to Jaffrey."

Todd's forehead wrinkled. "Why did you say, 'God willing'?"

"It's just an old habit I learned from my dad. It means if God lets me live we'll—"

Todd gripped my arm tightly. "Are you going to die?"

"No, no, Todd. It's just a saying."

Louise suddenly leaped to her feet. "Okay, gang, let's

clean this mess up and get dressed. We've all got a date for dinner in about an hour, and those nice waiters at The Orangerie don't like to be kept waiting."

The days all passed so swiftly that on the morning of our departure there were four very long faces in Rooms 212 and 214. While the bellboys were loading our luggage into the trunk of our rented car, I stopped at the desk and paid our bill. I was at the door, on the way out, when I realized that I still had the boys' room keys in my pocket. I retraced my steps, dropped the keys on the marble check-out counter, and turned.

"Mr. Christopher!"

The pretty desk clerk who had just processed my bill was holding an envelope in her hand. "Glad you came back. Forgot to give you this message that was in your box."

I stood immobile, staring down at the buff-colored envelope with my name written in small blue calligraphic letters. Finally, I tore it open, removed the gold-bordered card, and read:

> *Drink fully from the cup of joy.*
> *No man is more deserving than you.*
> *But prepare yourself mentally.*
> *Your moment of choice approaches swiftly.*

The card, like the first one, was signed *A. B. Salom.* None of the clerks could recall handling the envelope or placing it in my box. I crumbled both card and envelope into a ball and dropped it into a standing brass ashtray before stepping out into the blinding Phoenix sunlight.

XII

LATE IN MARCH, 1982, CHARLES BERGEN, ACCOMPANIED by David Coronet, president of Goliath Books, largest paperback publisher in the world, arrived unexpectedly at our front door. Charles lamely apologized for the surprise visit, but Louise and I were so happy to finally meet the guy that we welcomed him as if he were the prodigal son. Of course, it took us a little while to adjust to his appearance. Because of his perpetually hoarse voice and his speech patterns, as I have already mentioned, we had visualized an old man, and yet Charles was scarcely in his thirties, walked with the effortless ease of an athlete, wore tight-fitting designer jeans and a black cashmere jacket. Hardly the typical publisher's image.

David Coronet, on the other hand, was perfect casting. His slim waist tapered up to massive shoulders, slightly rounded, on which was perched a square-jawed, heavily lined face beneath a shock of pure white undisciplined hair. Even his dark blue pin-striped suit and deep baritone voice seemed perfectly in character for this legendary publishing genius who had built Goliath Books, almost single-handedly, into a publishing giant in less than twenty years.

Eventually, as with most of our visitors, the usual tour of house and grounds ended at the lighthouse, where Louise served us coffee and rolls before dashing off to pick up Glenn at high school.

David Coronet leaned back on the couch, unbuttoned his straining jacket, crossed his knees, and raised his cup above his head. "Marvelous—all of this! The Tower of Success! Perfectly named. Everything—the hilltop, your home, this lighthouse—just as so many articles have described them. And you and Louise, Mark, exactly as I hoped you would be, charming, unpretentious—truly down-to-earth. It's great to be here!"

"Thank you. It's an honor to have both of you drop in on us."

"I knew Joshua Croydon many years ago," the old publisher said. "Almost put out a whole series of his books for kids. He was a bright and talented man. Had much to say and said it well. And to think that all of his well-turned sentences originated here."

I pointed toward my desk. "That was his typewriter. A gift to me from his wife."

Coronet rose, walked slowly to the desk, and lightly tapped several keys on the Underwood. "And you wrote A Better Way to Live on this relic?"

"Every word."

"Amazing! Do you suppose that you could have written the same book on another typewriter and in another setting?"

That was a question no one had ever asked me.

"Well, I can't remember any occasion when the ghost of Joshua Croydon reached over my shoulder and tapped out a couple of paragraphs for me, if that's what you're suggesting. This was the man's studio, and that was his typewriter, but the book, I can assure you, is all mine. No co-author, especially a dead one."

The old man chuckled. "Forgive me. Goliath has been publishing so many books dealing with the occult lately that I'm beginning to see ghost-story plots under every street light. Silly. Tell me about that fascinating mail room of yours back at the house. How many fan letters are you receiving these days?"

"We seem to have settled down to around eight hundred a week."

He shook his head in wonder. "That's incredible when one considers that the book has been out, now, eighteen months. Any mail from 'crazies'?"

"A handful each week, but those we don't answer, although we do save them."

"Do they worry you?"

I hesitated. "They did at first, but we just laugh at them now. It's all part of the price, I guess, for this kind of fame or notoriety or whatever you want to call it."

At last Charles broke his prolonged silence. "Mark, it's so great to finally get to spend a little time with you, and how nice it is for me to discover, like David, that you're just the kind of man I hoped you would be. Of course, you realize that this visit, today, is not an accident."

I grinned. "You were not just passing through?"

He smiled nervously. "No, David and I have been meeting for several weeks in New York, discussing the possibility of Goliath Books purchasing the United States paperback rights to A Better Way to Live."

I turned to David Coronet. "I don't know very much

about publishing, especially the paperback side of it, but don't you usually have editors and attorneys who handle all the negotiating for reprint rights?"

"The very best in the business. But your publisher, here, is a tough cookie, and the hardcover copies of your book are still selling so well that he doesn't even want to discuss paperback rights. I've had two editors on his case for months, but they've thrown up their hands and dumped it all in my lap since they know how badly I want this book for Goliath. Mark, I asked Charles to bring me here so that I could have the opportunity to talk with you personally. I've come prepared to make you an offer that will set the publishing industry on its ear when the news gets out. The amount of money involved will far exceed any sum ever paid before as an advance against royalties for paperback rights to any book."

I turned to Charles and said, "I just don't understand. You've got the contractual power to arrange any subsidiary rights sales without checking with me. You've already sold many of the foreign rights and done a terrific job. Why are you consulting with me on this one?"

Charles leaned back, scratching his forehead. "Because this sale to Goliath, Mark, is contingent on your agreeing to certain activities in connection with the promotion of the paperback edition."

"You mean like going out on one of those insane publicity tours and hustling the book on every radio and television show in the country—is that what you're trying to tell me?"

Before Charles could reply, Coronet was on his feet. He removed his jacket and tossed it on the couch after taking a long cigar from an inside pocket. He lit the cigar and said, "Let me, very briefly, explain our proposed plans. May I?"

I shrugged and sat back.

"Mark, I truly believe you have written the greatest success book of all time. It's not just filled with a lot of theory and hokum, but concise and practical suggestions that everyone can follow to change their lives for the better. I want your book for Goliath badly enough so that I have already put my position on the line with our board of directors. I had to sell them first and I did. Here's what I propose. Our first printing will be the largest in publishing history, fifteen million copies! Your book will be distributed in every retail outlet in the country—grocery stores, drug stores, newsstands, bookstores, airports, department stores—displayed in special racks backed up by store posters and local commercials on radio and television. You will visit the twenty-four major metropolitan areas of this country, spending two days in each city appearing on the top television and radio shows in each market plus being interviewed by the press and autographing your book in the leading bookstores. You will be accompanied, in each city, by one of our representatives who will guide you through the day so that you'll have nothing to concern yourself about except being the charming Mark Christopher. At the end of your tour, after forty-eight days of promotion, your trip will climax with you delivering a speech based on your book to a packed crowd at Yankee Stadium. That speech will be carried, if we can work it out, by a major television network. Of course, we will attend to all the details of the entire tour and do our very best to see that you are not overworked along the way."

"Yankee Stadium?"

"Why not? This will be the biggest nonathletic event there since the Pope's visit, several years ago. We'll sell tickets and donate all the proceeds to your favorite charity.

Might even be able to engineer a ticker-tape parade down Broadway—or up Broadway. All of it!"

Charles leaned toward me. "Mark, Goliath's paperback edition will reach the millions who can't afford ten dollars for a hardcover copy of any book, and those are just the people who need your book the most. You'll do more, through the mass distribution of your principles, to lift our country out of its apathy and self-pity and concern about the future than any Congress and President combined. I believe it."

"You're starting to sound like a carnival barker, Charles. This is just a book, for God's sake. It's not 'The Sermon on the Mount, Part Two.' "

"It is not *just* a book," Coronet interrupted. "It happens to be, I'm convinced, the best self-help book ever written—a magnificent road map to a better life for anyone who will follow your precepts, Mark. Look, I know how much you love your two boys and Louise. That comes through in every article I read about you. Forget about us, forget about your public, forget about yourself, and just think of your family for a minute. If you agree to my terms, you'll be able to insure that they will never want for much no matter what happens in the future. How much is that worth to you? Is fifty days out of your life, spreading the gospel according to Christopher around this country, too big a price to pay?"

Charles was staring down at the tips of his Gucci loafers. His head was tilted as if he were waiting for the executioner's axe to fall. My axe.

"David," I heard myself saying, "what's the record advance paid for the paperback rights to a hardcover bestseller?"

The old man rubbed his chin and replied, "Slightly over three million dollars."

I gulped. "Three million? . . ."

David placed his hand on my shoulder and said, "Goliath Books is prepared to pay considerably more for *A Better Way to Live.*"

I took a deep breath. "How much?"

"Five million dollars!"

XIII

LEAVING TODD AND GLENN IN MARY MELLON'S CARE, Louise and I drove down to Boston and flew to New York, two weeks later, for Goliath's black-tie press party at the New York Hilton announcing their acquisition of the paperback rights to *A Better Way to Live.* Goliath's publicity department had moved swiftly and thoroughly as soon as the contract had been signed. When Louise and I finally entered the hotel's grand ballroom, flanked by David Coronet and Charles Bergen, we were greeted by a cheering capacity crowd, flashing cameras, and a frightening bank of television lights.

Louise, smiling and waving at the cameras, still managed to nudge me softly with her elbow and said, "Well, you've certainly gotten us into quite a mess this time!"

"Just keep smiling, my love. You're doing fine."

"My God, Mark, there's Lauren Bacall and . . . and Charlton Heston and the mayor . . . what's his name?"

"Koch. Maybe he's brought us the key to New York City."

"I'd rather have a hot pastrami on rye. I'm starved."

"Serves you right. You just picked at your dinner."

"I was nervous. Why aren't you nervous?"

"I am. I'm just too numb for it to show. Keep smiling now. That a girl. . . ."

Eventually, David and Charles managed to maneuver us through the sea of outstretched hands to the center of the ballroom where a huge ice sculpture of the Tower of Success, bathed in amber spotlights from above, was surrounded by tables manned by an army of bartenders pouring champagne.

David handed us each an empty goblet and poured from a full magnum of Dom Perignon, but before the sparkling liquid touched any of our lips we had to pose for endless photographs with our glasses raised in toast. Finally, he said, "Well, I think it's about time. Stand by, while I greet our impressive gathering of celebrities, reporters, and freeloaders."

Some men are born to wear a tuxedo, and David Coronet is one of them. Standing ramrod straight at the single microphone on the ballroom's low stage, he looked like the chairman of the board of the entire world. He waited calmly, hands clasped in front of him, until the room quieted down.

"Friends, I welcome all of you. This is an important night in the history of Goliath Books and, indeed, in American book publishing. I am proud to announce, as most of you already know, that Goliath has purchased the United States reprint rights to a book that has, in less than two years, become the bestselling hardcover book of all time in this country."

He paused. Perhaps ten seconds. "But what none of

you know, until this very moment, is that the purchase price, the advance against royalties for *A Better Way to Live*, has never before been approached in the entire forty-three years that paperbacks have existed as we know them today . . . five million dollars!"

The old man paused again. This time he had no choice. A loud roar erupted from the standing crowd, a combination of sounds ranging from astonishment to admiration to envy, punctuated by whistles and shrieks. Suddenly, I felt as if everyone in the ballroom was staring at me, and I could feel Louise moving very close to me.

David Coronet finally could be heard again. "Goliath's first printing will be another record breaker, fifteen million copies. Already three of our printing plants are gearing up for around-the-clock production in order to have all of those copies in every possible retail outlet in the nation by August 11 when Mark Christopher begins a national promotional tour that will take him to the twenty-four major marketing areas in this country. Those of you with press kits will find a list of the cities and the approximate dates when he will appear in each, on radio and television and meeting with the press, along with a select number of autograph parties in the larger stores. You might also be interested to know that the mayors of every city on his tour have already graciously agreed to designate his first day in their city as 'Mr. Success Day,' and all of this will culminate, after forty-eight days, with Mr. Christopher appearing as the featured speaker, along with an impressive supporting cast, in a giant *Better Way to Live* rally at Yankee Stadium, on September 28, with all the proceeds going to charity."

The applause continued for what seemed an interminable length of time before David raised his right hand. "Ladies and gentlemen, as you all have read. Mr. Christopher rarely ventures very far from his hilltop home and his beloved lighthouse in New Hampshire, that symbol of hope that we have all come to know as the Tower of Success. However, we're most honored to have him here tonight—"

"For five million bucks, how could he stay away?" a male voice shouted from a nearby group, and the throng roared with laughter, including David, until he raised his hand again.

"We're most honored to have him with us, this evening, accompanied by his lovely wife, and I thought that perhaps he might like to come up here and say a few words to you. Please remember this is not a press conference. Hold your questions, and if you'd like an interview with our distinguished author, after you have reviewed the press kit, kindly contact Goliath's publicity department. We'll make every effort to arrange one at some convenient future date. And now, friends, it gives me great pleasure to introduce Mr. Success, himself . . . Mark Christopher!"

The applause increased in decibels as I mounted the stage, approached the microphone, and shook David's hand. Momentarily blinded by the television lights, I waited nervously, bowing my head and trying to smile at the dark void in front of me, still not certain what I was going to say.

"Ladies and gentlemen, all of us, I imagine, start out on this uncertain road of life with a dream, an ambition, a goal. A fortunate few manage to survive all the hazards, roadblocks, and potholes along the way to reach their objectives. Most of us, however, get sidetracked on our journey and stumble through our allotted years with our hopes and dreams eventually fading even from our memory. For me, this is the realization of a dream that was buried with my blessed mother, twenty-five years ago."

The ballroom had become very still.

"Tonight, by your very presence here, you do honor not to me but to her . . . and to her dream. And Mom, wherever you are, I'm sorry that it took me so long, but I just want you to know that your kid finally made it."

Hours later, with the champagne still flowing for those reluctant to challenge a rainy New York night, David and Charles walked us to the elevator doors, both promising to call us in the morning before we headed for LaGuardia Airport and home. Riding up in the elevator, Louise sighed, "Hon, I'm so proud of you. You were wonderful with the people."

I held up my right hand. It was throbbing. "Wonder how many hands I shook?"

"I don't know, but I'm afraid it's only the beginning."

"Hope I survive."

"You will . . . and when that tour is over, we'll have you back with us, and it will be just like old times. All this hoopla will eventually end. Even national heroes get pushed aside for a fresh crop of idols every season or so."

I turned the hotel key in the door to our suite and held it open for Louise. "Oh Mark," she exclaimed, pointing to a large basket of fruit wrapped tightly in cellophane, sitting on the square coffee table, "wasn't that nice of the hotel?"

She kicked off her shoes, hurried toward the fruit and then backed away. "Mark!"

"What's the matter?"

"Look!"

A square, buff-colored envelope rested against the side of the basket. On it was my name inscribed in blue calligraphy. I tore it open and scanned the brief message on the gold-bordered card before handing it to Louise:

91

Mr. Christopher, your mother is well aware that you have scaled the pinnacle. The bond between parents and their children endures for all eternity. This you must not forget when you are asked to render your choice. I shall consult with you soon.

A. B. Salom.

Louise angrily kicked at the basket of fruit and sent it crashing to the floor. "Mark, whoever wrote this note was in the ballroom tonight and heard you talking about your mother! I'm frightened."

I couldn't keep it from her any longer. Holding her close, I told her about the second message that I had received as we were leaving the Arizona Biltmore.

"We've got to put a stop to this," she sobbed. "It's not like the crazy stuff we keep getting in the mail at home. This person is *following* us! Somehow he, or she, managed to get that first letter into one of the mailbags in New Hampshire. Then he left you a note at the hotel desk in Arizona. And now this! Why? Maybe you should tell David when he calls tomorrow . . . or the F.B.I. . . . somebody. We need help. We've got to find out what this Absalom wants before he drives us crazy."

The skin on my neck began to crawl. "What did you just say? Find out what *who* wants?"

"Absalom."

"Louise, the sender of these weird notes signs his name A. B. Salom."

"So? How do *you* pronounce A. B. Salom?"

"Absalom?"

"See!"

"Absalom, Absalom. Sounds biblical."

"It is biblical," she said. "Absalom, I remember from my Sunday school days, was a son of King David . . . but that's all I recall."

"Do you suppose there's some kind of clue in the name?"

"Who knows? What we do know, for certain, is that our mysterious messenger was in this hotel tonight. He was probably even in this room, dear God! I'll bet if you check, downstairs, they'll have no record of a delivery here, this evening."

I phoned the hotel desk. Louise was correct. By the time I placed the phone back on its cradle, she was furiously turning the pages of a Gideon Bible she had discovered in the drawer of our nightstand. Finally, she paused and began to read, her wide eyes darting back and forth across the pages. I waited for what seemed an eternity before she closed the Bible gently.

"Well?"

She looked away. "I was right, Mark. Absalom was a son of David."

Silence. Minutes passed. "And??" I prodded impatiently.

"He led a revolt against his father and was killed by one of David's generals. When the king was notified of his son's death, he cried out, in grief, 'O Absalom, my son, my son. . . . Would I had died for thee, O Absalom, my son!'"

XIV

WE WERE AT LEAST HALFWAY BACK TO BOSTON, ON Eastern's Flight 23, before Louise slapped at my knee and broke what had been, for us, a long and very rare period of gloomy silence.

"Hey, aren't we something? Anyone would think that we were returning from a funeral instead of having been honored by the cream of the publishing world less than twenty-four hours ago. We should be two of the happiest people in the world. You are about to receive more money than we can ever spend; your name has become a household word, not only here but abroad; celebrities ask *you* for autographs; millions honor you and love you for your book—and look at us! We've let three notes from some creep rain on our parade and spoil the most important happening of our lives!"

"That's not what you were saying last night after you place-kicked the fruit basket."

"I know," she nodded, "but after the wonderful high of the reception, it wasn't easy trying to deal with another message from the twilight zone."

"And now you're no longer worried?"

"Of course I'm worried. But I've decided that I'm not going to allow someone I don't even know to push my mood buttons and direct how I feel. You wrote about that—how we relinquish our own sovereignty whenever we let the words and actions of others force us to think or say or do things that are incompatible with our personality. That never has to happen if we guard against it, right?"

"Right. When you let anybody dump on you, then you are putting your life in their hands, and the price you always pay for permitting that to happen is very high."

"I knew that, but I guess I forgot it for a little while. By the way, when Charles and David called, this morning, did you tell them about our mysterious correspondent?"

"No, I didn't see much sense in worrying them."

"So what are we going to do about this little problem?"

"Something I probably should have done when we returned from our Arizona vacation."

Stephen and Sheila Hammond had been next-door neighbors during our last year in Brookline. Since the day their moving van arrived from Memphis, following Steve's transfer, our relationship had grown until they had become very close and dear friends. Originally, we were told only that Steve worked for the government, and I remember that several months passed before he and Sheila finally confided that he was the new head of the Boston field division of the Federal Bureau of Investigation. For many reasons, Steve explained, F.B.I. personnel preferred that their occupation and their home addresses not become general public knowledge, and neither Louise nor I ever violated his trust in us, even to our children.

After our plane landed at Logan Airport, I phoned Steve and hit the jackpot. He was in his office, would be there for the entire afternoon, and would love to see his old neighbors again.

We spent more than two hours with Steve in his large corner office at the John F. Kennedy Federal Office Building. Beginning with our discovery of the first calligraphic note in a mailbag, we told him what little there was to tell while he made notes on a long legal pad. By the time we had finished, that old familiar smile had all but vanished from his face. Finally, he pointed to the card and envelope we had found in our room at the Hilton and stared at it for the umpteenth time.

"That first card and envelope, Mark, are they still tacked on your bulletin board in that celebrated Tower of Success?"

"They were when we left."

"Will you send them to me?"

"Sure."

"I'd like to have the lab run a few tests on both notes and envelopes. Also, may we take your fingerprints and Louise's? Maybe we can dig up a stray print on these things that doesn't belong to either one of you."

"Anything you suggest, Steve. What do you think? What's this all about? You must have plenty of experience with this sort of thing."

"Frankly, kids, I don't know what to think. I've had some success tracking down senders of extortion notes, but this stuff is in another league. Not easy to classify. Kook mail, of course, just comes with the territory. Presidents, movie stars, and more and more sports personalities, lately, are recipients. Most of it is easy to ignore. You said you get a lot of it yourself, but Louise touched on an important point when she said that this particular individual must be following you. He had to have been in New Hampshire to place that unaddressed and unstamped envelope in the mailbag; he was in Phoenix to leave the second note for you at the desk; and he was probably in your room at the Hilton last night. Of course, with all the publicity you've been getting, especially about the money your book is earning, the easy first possibility that comes to mind is kidnapping. And the references in these notes to your having to make some kind of a choice soon, Mark, could involve how you would or would not handle a ransom demand. But please, Louise, don't look so alarmed. I don't think this has anything to do with a kidnapping, either of one of you or the kids. I can't remember a single case where the kidnapper warned his victims *before* the act was committed. No . . . this note, and from what you have told me of the contents of the other two, almost seems to be from a friend who is trying to *warn* you about something that is still ahead of you."

"Some friend. Then you don't think much of Louise's Absalom theory and a possible message in the name itself?"

He shrugged his thin shoulders. "Sounds too much like an old hidden clue Ellery Queen mystery for my taste. But I don't know. Could be anything. We've got some strange people walking around out there. Some of them send Valentines that explode, others mail packages of dog droppings, some even put LSD in the candy they pass out to little kids on Halloween."

Louise joined in. "What about our kids, Steve? I don't want to frighten them unnecessarily. Do we tell them? Do we hire guards, for God's sake? Go into hiding? How do we handle this? What should we do?"

"I wouldn't do anything for now," he said, holding up the gold-bordered card by its edge. "I know it's easy to say and tough to do, but I'd try to put it all out of my mind and go on with your lives. This last note closes with the sentence, 'I shall consult with you soon.' Apparently whatever decision that Mark is going to have to make will be presented to him by this individual in person. If that happens, Mark, I want you to call me as soon as you can after you have been approached."

I forced a laugh. "If I'm able to . . ."

He continued as if he hadn't heard me. "Contact me immediately. If I'm not here, they'll know where to find me. You both got that? And if the lab can learn anything from this card and the other one, I'll give you a call, pronto."

"Steve," I asked, "how about the calligraphy? Does that mean anything?"

"Not really. Calligraphy is in. Everybody is using it. Sheila, right now, is going to a class once a week to learn how to write pretty like this card. She figures it will be a classy way to sign our Christmas cards. Oh, and speaking of signing things . . ."

He pulled open the middle drawer of his desk and withdrew a copy of *A Better Way to Live*. "Will you please autograph this for Sheila and me? I can't tell you how much it's helped us handle a few personal problems in the last year or so. Never realized that my neighbor who was always burning his steaks on the barbecue grill and couldn't hammer a nail had so much wisdom and talent. One never knows."

I inscribed the book to both of them, with love, and passed it back. Our hands touched for a moment, and he said, with compassion, "This being Mr. Success can be hell, huh Mark?"

XV

DURING THE LATE SPRING AND EARLY SUMMER OF 1982, our hilltop home became a virtual hermitage at my request. David Coronet and his people at Goliath Books, who had assumed total responsibility for the promotion and publicizing of *A Better Way to Live* from Charles Bergen, cooperated magnificently. I had asked David for three peaceful months with my family before beginning the terrible grind of fifty days on the road, figuring I would need all of that time, at least, to prepare myself mentally for the ordeal. He agreed reluctantly, after making several attempts to change my mind, and the media people suddenly ceased beating a daily path to the Tower of Success.

David also informed me that ABC had signed to televise my portion of the Yankee Stadium affair on September 28 and that my speech should be no more than twenty-three minutes in length since they were planning a thirty-minute special that was to air in the east at ten-thirty on that Tuesday night. An impressive lineup of motivational speakers had already agreed to appear on the program prior to my televised spot, and when I heard their names I wondered how on earth I would ever be able to follow such powerhouses.

Soon I began spending my tranquil mornings on the difficult task of trying to condense the contents of *A Better Way to Live* down to an oral presentation of less than four thousand words for the Yankee Stadium speech without neglecting any of its more important principles. Not easy. Later, I would be grateful for this forced exercise in brevity since the notes that I made on each chapter in order to shape my talk became great memory joggers that I took with me on tour and reviewed each morning before facing the radio, television, and press people in each city.

Louise and Glenn, obviously working in collusion, did everything in their power to keep my mind off the countdown to August 11, when the tour was scheduled to begin, but Todd innocently pushed the perfect diversionary button for me at breakfast one morning late in April. Little League tryouts and practices were scheduled to commence in less than three weeks, and although I had decided that I would not manage or coach a team, because of my schedule, I was still looking forward to watching my growing athlete, whenever possible, enjoy an even better year than 1981 when he had played sixteen games at second base on my team with only two errors and had batted .525, including four legitimate home runs.

"Dad," he said, pushing aside his cereal bowl and waiting until he had my undivided attention, "I'm trying out for pitcher this year."

"Todd, you're the best second baseman in the league. Why are you switching now, for heaven's sake?"

"I've always wanted to pitch, Dad."

"How come you never told me?"

"Because . . ." he hesitated, searching the open palm of his right hand for the proper words, "because I played on your team last year, and I didn't want the other kids to think that—that—"

"You didn't want the other kids to think that because you were my son and I was coaching the team, you were getting special treatment if I let you pitch?"

He nodded and looked at me pleadingly with those large brown eyes. "But this year you're not coaching, and I'd like to try. Will you help me?"

"You know I will. Any way that I can. What do you want me to do?"

"I'd like to throw to you, every afternoon, in the yard. I need a lot of work on my control, and I'd like you to teach me how to throw a change-up."

"You're really serious about this?"

"Yes, I am."

"I'll work your butt off. You'll have to practice harder than you ever have before. Are you willing to pay the price?"

"I'm willing, Dad. I know that nothing worth achieving comes easy in this life."

Louise almost choked on her toast. "Where did you learn that, Todd?" she gasped.

"I'm reading Dad's book, Mom."

That very same day, while Todd was in school, I drove to the largest sporting goods store in Concord and made several purchases. By the time he came home I had constructed a raised pitching mound, complete with a regulation pitching rubber, on the south side of the Tower of Success. And exactly forty-six feet away, the official Little

League distance, rested a shiny white five-sided home plate.

Our practice sessions began immediately. For the first few days we worked only on Todd's pitching motion and delivery until he learned to utilize his entire body instead of just his arm to generate throwing speed. Gradually, his control improved, and after a week I had him throwing fifty pitches a day to me while I called balls and strikes. He began working on his change-up after ten days, pitching with the same overhand delivery as his fast ball but pulling his hand back as he released the baseball so that it came up to the plate with only two-thirds the velocity of his fast ball. Like most boys his age he also wanted to try throwing a curve, but I finally convinced him that if he could control his fast ball and mix it with an occasional change-up, he could probably get any kid out.

Each day my ambitious offspring improved, and as his control got better, his confidence rose. Most important, he listened to my coaching and worked diligently at correcting whatever I may have noticed he was doing wrong. Our time together, every afternoon, became the highlight of my day after working in the lighthouse each morning on my speech. I was twelve years old, once again, and I joined him often in his journeys through the glorious world of baseball fantasy, the same unforgettable trips that I had once taken with my father.

"Come on, hot shot," I would yell as I squatted behind the plate, my glove poised, "it's the seventh game of the World Series. You've got a one-run lead. We're in the last of the ninth, there are two out, the bases are loaded, and you've just come in from the bullpen to face Reggie Jackson. Now—let's see you work on him!"

With jaw set and forehead wrinkled, Todd would

stare ferociously down from the mound for my signal, tug firmly on his Los Angeles Dodger blue cap, start his pumping motion, rear back and fire.

"Strike one!"

"Stri-i-ke two!"

"Ball one."

He'd shake his head, unhappy at the call, turn his back on me and gaze out at his imaginary outfield. Finally, he'd return to the mound, scowl in my direction, bend low at the waist, swing both arms behind him and over his head and . . . thump!

"Strike thre-e-e-e!"

Then I would toss my glove high in the air and rush to the mound to embrace and congratulate our World Series hero.

"I told you I could be a pitcher, Dad!" he would cry as he leaped into my arms and kissed me, an act not usually seen at Anaheim or Dodger Stadium. "Thank you for helping me. I love you!"

"I love you too, son, and I'm very proud of you. I think you're going to make it."

"I'll pitch a no-hitter for you this year. Just wait and see."

I am convinced that the greatest legacy we can leave our children are happy memories: those precious moments so much like pebbles on the beach that are plucked from the white sand and placed in tiny boxes that lay undisturbed on tall shelves until one day they spill out and time repeats itself, with joy and sweet sadness, in the child now an adult. Would Todd recall our special afternoons together on some early spring day, perhaps twenty years from now, when his own young son tosses a baseball at him for the first time? Memories. Love's best preservative.

Quite often, while we were going through our workouts, Louise would come out of the house to applaud her two ballplayers. One afternoon, after we had finished, Todd rode off on his bicycle with his glove and bat, in search of more action, while the two of us relaxed on a bench in the lengthening shadow from the lighthouse.

"You're breathing hard, coach," she teased.

"So would you be if you had to bend your knees and squat fifty times while trying to protect yourself from a small, very hard object heading for your head at more than fifty miles an hour."

She giggled and rested her cheek on my damp shoulder. Louise and I had grown even closer to each other, if such a thing were possible, as the departure date for my tour approached. After several minutes of silence she finally asked, "Mark, who is Alexander Anthony? I feel as if I should know that name, but I've come up blank."

"Why are you asking about Anthony?"

"You tell me about him, first, and then I'll tell you why."

"Okay, Alexander Anthony was a war correspondent during the second World War. After the war he wrote a smash bestseller called How to Conquer Life which has become a classic in success literature. If I were ever pinned down to select the very best self-help book ever written, it would be his. Also, he never wrote another book."

Louise slapped at her forehead with the palm of her hand. "What a dummy I am! Of course. You often mentioned him in your company speeches, and there's a section about his principles of success in A Better Way to Live, right?"

"Right. Anthony is also a mystery man. After all the fame he achieved from the book, and he was the toast of two continents for several years, he suddenly dropped out of sight never to be heard from again. There were hundreds of articles written about his strange disappearance, and he became the most famous missing person since Amelia Earhart until the public eventually forgot all about him. If he were still alive, he'd be well over seventy. . . ."

"I think he's still alive, Mark," Louise said haltingly as she handed me a postcard. "This came in today's mail."

The tiny handwriting was shaky but legible. The writer admired my book and appreciated the kind words I had written about him. He would like me to visit with him, and he was only twenty miles away in Stoddard. I could come when I pleased since he was always at home. Directions to locate his cabin followed. The card was signed *Alexander Anthony*.

I rubbed my fingers gently over the signature. "I can't believe this, Louise. It's like getting a message from the grave. The one person in the world I would most like to talk with, and learn from—who I was certain had died long ago, has just invited me to his home. Why me? And where has he been all these years? This man's book changed millions of lives, and it's still doing it. But maybe it's just a gag. Another nut playing games with us."

"I don't think so, Mark. I've got a hunch that his postcard is for real, and because of your book he obviously feels he has a kindred spirit in you that he can trust. Like it or not, you've become a magnet, and all sorts of people are attracted to you because you have touched them so deeply with your words. You just can't hide from it, and you can't run from it. Someday soon I'm afraid that you're going to have to deal with A. B. Salom, whoever he is. But for now Alexander Anthony sounds like a lonely man who needs you. If his book and his words have meant so much to you, then you have no choice. When are you going to see him?"

"A wild goose chase, for sure."

She kept staring at me, saying nothing.

"Tomorrow," I promised.

XVI

THE DIRECTIONS ON THE POSTCARD WERE PERFECT. ON my first pass along Route 123, as it meandered through the tiny village of Stoddard, I managed to locate the narrow dirt road picturesquely named Birch Point Lane and bumped along its rutted surface for exactly half a mile. Then I turned right through the only opening in the thicket of tall blueberry bushes flanking the road and followed car tracks almost hidden beneath pine needles that led me down to a stained, clapboard house only a few yards from the shoreline of a small body of tranquil water called Island Pond.

Near the house's open porch that faced toward the water, a tall, gaunt, bearded man, flanked by two piles of split logs, leaned on his axe handle and stared intently as my newly purchased 1982 Jeep Wagoneer approached. Finally, his mouth opened wide, the axe slid from his grasp, and the Lincolnesque figure limped hurriedly toward my car while rubbing his hands against his faded jeans and plaid flannel shirt.

He arrived at my side just as I closed the car door, reaching out to me with both arms and shouting, in the most captivating basso profundo voice I have ever heard, "You must be none other than the great Mark Christopher! I welcome you to my humble retreat."

I thought I had prepared myself mentally, during the drive from Jaffrey, for the long shot possibility that I might, indeed, meet Alexander Anthony in person, but now that he was actually shaking my hand it still took several minutes for me to collect myself.

"Sir," I finally sputtered, "I can't tell you what a great honor this is for me . . . and shock. I was certain you were dead."

His full lips, scarcely visible beneath his white beard and mustache, arched into a faint smile. "There are many ways to die, Mr. Christopher, many ways. Let us go inside and visit, shall we?"

I'm certain there are logging camps deep in the Allagash wilderness of Maine that have more amenities. The old man led me through his small kitchen, its floor covered by worn linoleum, past an old black Franklin wood stove, a round table covered with faded oilcloth, two paint-chipped pale green chairs, and a soapstone sink stacked with dishes. His living room, as he called it, was paneled with rough, unpainted pine slabs, and its squeaking floorboards were partially covered by a frayed, braided rug on which rested a flimsy coffee table straining to support a small mountain of newspapers and magazines. Surrounding the table were two overstuffed chairs and a sofa whose armrests had been worn down to its wooden frames. Against one wall stood a giant fieldstone fireplace looking completely out of place in such shabby surroundings. And everywhere there were books—books piled high in irregular columns, some almost reaching to the unpainted Sheetrock ceiling.

I sipped on the cool glass of cider he had brought from the kitchen, desperately groping for the correct words to cover the embarrassment I felt at finding my long-time hero in such grim surroundings. Wasn't necessary. Facing me as he sat on the edge of the sofa, Alexander Anthony was about to make no apologies for the condition of his habitat. Instead, he gracefully raised his glass toward mine until they touched and said enthusiastically, "I salute your marvelous book and its brilliant creator! You should be very proud."

"I am, sir, but I owe so much to you. Your great book guided me through many tough years and many good ones. The good ones, I'm learning, can be as difficult to handle as the bad ones. I don't know what my life would be like today if I hadn't followed the principles of living I learned from you. You taught me how to cope with the world, but more important, you taught me how to cope with myself."

The old man lowered his head. "You are very kind. Even after all these years it is good to hear such words again. Vanity is an almost incurable disease, I'm afraid. But Mark, if I may call you Mark, I've had many years to think about my single literary effort, and I've just about come to the conclusion that books such as ours, success books if you will, do not deserve all the fuss that is often made over them. They become fads, styles of the moment, and have little or no lasting effect on humanity. Our books, filled with hope and encouragement, seem to be little more than aspirin tablets for headaches that never go away."

"With all due respect, sir, I just can't agree with

you. In the past year or so I've received thousands of letters . . ."

He winced. "Ah yes, the letters. I remember them. Forgive me, son, but I'm afraid that you have only touched most of your readers for perhaps a day or a week or a month. They write to you at the height of their elation, while your powerfully written ideas are still fresh in their minds. Momentarily, you may have convinced them that they can be better than they are. But their renewed hope rarely survives their next failure, and they soon come to realize that they are not equipped to become champion race horses but must spend their days, instead, straining at plowshares in order to survive."

I began to respond, but he raised his hand. "Eventually, Mark, all books such as ours end up on bookshelves, gathering dust and forgotten, while their once enthusiastic owners continue to lead what Thoreau so aptly called 'lives of quiet desperation.' They give up on themselves. They quit trying. And why should we expect any more from the vast majority of mankind? After all, the greatest instruction book of all has been with us, in one form or another, for thousands of years, and we still act more like animals than angels."

He waved at the newspapers on the coffee table. "Even now, as you and I talk, people are killing each other in Afghanistan, Iran, Iraq, Northern Ireland, Cambodia, Namibia, Chad, Guatemala, Lebanon, El Salvador, and Ethiopia—not to mention all the other terrible crimes that take place, daily, in every city and town in the world. We steal from each other. We cheat on each other. We brutalize each other. We crawl over each other in our race for power, wealth, and fame. What good is it for believers like you and me to spell out a long list of success principles that we know will work, that we know will guide people to a better life if they follow them, when they can't even obey ten simple commandments. We light candles in the darkness, but we manage to attract only moths. So why should we try? Why should we make any attempt to rescue this human race that may not even be worth saving?"

I couldn't believe what I was hearing. Dale Carnegie advising me to insult everyone I meet or Norman Vincent Peale preaching the benefits of negative thinking wouldn't have been as shocking. What had happened to my idol? Had the long years he had hidden from the world poisoned him so completely, or was he just testing me, playing the devil's advocate with his harsh condemnation of man in order to unveil, through my response, either my sincerity or my phoniness? Whichever it was, I had to answer him. For my own sake. I knew that in a few weeks, on my publicity tour, I would be defending myself against similar arguments from many interviewers in all twenty-four cities. I was fair game to be challenged, and having the top bestseller for so long made me a perfect target for any talk-show host with a mean streak.

I drained my glass of cider before responding. "Alex, I don't know if the human race is worth saving, and fortunately, I don't have to make that decision. But I do know that there are many humans worth salvaging. For every murderer you point out to me, I'll find you at least one individual who gave his or her life to save another, often a stranger. For every thief you finger, I'll show you a thousand caring people who wouldn't steal a slice of bread even if their bellies were empty. Inside every living person is a very special ingredient. We've never seen it, we've never touched it, we've never been able to locate it. But it's there—and I'm convinced that it was put there by God. We've given that special ingredient many names through the years—soul, spirit, light, flame, but what we call it is not important so long as we realize that we have it—a special gift, a gift from God. The trouble is that this mysterious force, whatever name you hang on it, is dormant in the majority of humans, usually through no fault of their own. It's a damn tough world out there, and many of us can't deal with it very well, especially after we've been knocked down again and again. How many times can one fail before deciding never to try again? How many times does a kid have to hear that he or she will never make it in this life before he or she accepts that verdict, usually from a parent or teacher, and spends the rest of his or her days fulfilling the prophecy of failure? And yet that special, invisible something inside each of us is what prevents our condition from ever becoming hopeless so long as there is a breath of life in us. The most important function that books like yours and mine accomplish is a revival of that ebbing spirit. We unlock the cell door for millions who had resigned themselves to a life that is no life at all. No, Alex, we can't save them all, but even the greatest teacher who ever walked this earth couldn't do that, so why should we be disappointed with lesser results? We can only try. What's it worth to our world if we can rescue just one person from the misery of failure and help him or her reach full potential? Isn't that enough reward for anyone? I know it is for me."

The lines around the old man's pale blue eyes seemed to soften, and his head nodded, almost imperceptibly. "Thank you. I just wanted to hear you say it," he said faintly. "You are a good man, Mark, and I beg your forgiveness for provoking you in order to hear you speak from the heart. If it is of any consequence to you, I believe exactly as you do. Men and women may have their roots in the ground, and often those roots are starved and ravaged, yet there is not a human alive who cannot reach up and touch, with his or her fingers, the very top of God's rainbow. You and I, my friend, have only tried to show them how. The rest is up to them."

We spoke of many things in the next several hours. Of love, of hope, of failure, of death, of success, of children, of ambition, of authors, even of politics. Not until late in the afternoon, with the setting sun's rays reflecting off the placid pond against the room's ceiling, did I finally muster enough courage to ask him the question that had hovered unspoken between us since we had first met.

"Mr. Anthony . . . Alex . . . what happened to you? You had it all: fame, money, veneration by the public, success. The world was yours. You were a shining messenger of hope to a world licking their wounds after the most terrible war in history. And then you suddenly vanished. Why? Why did you toss it all away when you were standing where almost everyone dreams of standing, on the very top of the mountain?"

He sighed and tugged nervously on his long, gnarled fingers. "Difficult questions, Mark. And the answers are even tougher. But then, I did invite you here, didn't I?"

"I'm sorry, sir. We don't have to talk about it. It's just that I have felt so close to you, for so many years, that I just had to ask."

"No, no—you were kind enough to accept my invitation, and so I feel I have a special obligation to tell you, even though I've never discussed any of this with a single person in the past thirty-five years."

He stared up at the fading streaks of sunlight, inhaled deeply, and said, "I didn't toss it all away, Mark, I let it all slip through my fingers because of my own stupidity. I was able to tell everyone else how to deal with life and win, and yet I couldn't handle my own success."

"What happened?"

"Marge and I were married during the Depression, in 1934, while I was still a cub reporter for the Associated Press. A year later God blessed us with a beautiful son, and Marge insisted, against my protests, that we name him Alexander. We were living in Syracuse when the war broke out, and then we were apart for almost three years while I covered just about every major battle in Europe. I returned home to a brave and wonderful lady who had managed to keep things together and a ten-year-old who was almost a complete stranger. But that didn't last long. Baseball reunited us. Little League was just getting off the ground in those days but Alex managed to make one of the new teams as a pitcher and we worked together, almost every day that I was home, on his throwing."

I smiled. "Sounds familiar. Todd, my youngest, and I are going through the same routine every afternoon."

"Best days of my life, Mark."

"I know. Me too."

"I wrote *How to Conquer Life* in the evenings and weekends, basing it on the unbelievable acts of courage and will to survive I had witnessed among so many brave men in combat. Sold it to the first publisher I sent it to and it became an instant bestseller, changing my life completely in the process. Even though this was long before the kind of book promoting that goes on today, with all your radio and television talk shows, I still became a celebrity overnight. I even toured the country in a private railroad car, at the publisher's expense, making personal appearances at movie houses, autographing books for record crowds in all the best stores, and also giving interviews to the radio and press people. I loved all of it, especially the adulation of the masses. Many would grasp my hand and kiss it, after I had signed their books, wonderful simple people with tears in their eyes, thanking me again and again for saving their lives. It was all just too much for a simple country boy, even one who had seen a pretty good hunk of this crazy world. And the women. My, my! I fought that temptation for a long time, but I could feel myself gradually weakening during the extended trips away from home alone. Finally, I succumbed. They were all so lovely, and so willing to be with a famous author, and my family was far away. Actually, after a while, I was able to shut my wife and son completely out of my mind, with the help of booze. I was even smoking pot long before it became so fashionable. Fun. Fun and games . . . and since everyone had me convinced that I was bigger than life, I was positive that I could handle all of it. Until my wife flew to San Francisco on a surprise visit, to celebrate our wedding anniversary, and found me in bed at the Fairmont Hotel with a young actress who later became quite a famous movie star. Marge filed suit for divorce, very discreetly, and, of course, won custody of Alex."

"Was any of this ever in the papers?"

"No, but at considerable expense to my publisher, I'm sure, who was only trying to protect his investment. News of a divorce on moral grounds, in those days, would have ruined future book sales. But I didn't need a scandal to wipe out all the good I had accomplished. I proceeded to ruin myself. I just couldn't handle the divorce, couldn't accept losing Marge and Alex, especially since I knew in my heart that I didn't deserve to be a part of their lives after the way I had mistreated their love and faith in me. The toboggan slide from there was swift and final. I spent many nights in drunk tanks, almost lost my life in a couple of bar brawls, and gradually just dropped out of the world that had been so good to me. I never wrote another word for publication. How could I and be honest with myself after what I had done? The man who had produced *How to Conquer Life* let life conquer him. He fell from the top of the pile down to the gutter, and he has been doing his own brand of penance ever since. You see, Mark, Alexander Anthony didn't vanish nor did he just fade away. He drowned in brooze, humiliation, and self-pity."

I reached over and grasped his trembling hands. "Does anyone around here know who you are?"

He shook his head, looking more like a little boy lost than a broken old man.

"Does anyone at all who was important to you know that you are alive and well? Your publisher?"

"No."

"They must owe you a fortune in royalty payments. Your book is still selling well, you know."

"I could never bring myself to accept any of that money. I don't deserve it."

"This place. It's yours?"

"All mine. Bought it cheap, years ago."

"You must freeze in the winter. There doesn't seem to be much insulation."

"Well, it does get a mite nippy, as they say in this part of the world, but I survive."

"And how do you support yourself since you're probably not even collecting Social Security payments?"

"Odd jobs."

"Alex, you never saw your wife and son again?"

"Never. I heard that Marge remarried . . ."

"And your boy?"

He shut his eyes. "Alex was killed in Korea early in 1953."

He stood, limped to the fireplace, removed an object from the heavy mantel, returned and placed it in my hand. "This is all I have of my son. It is my most precious possession—far more valuable than my life."

I was holding a baseball, a Little League baseball, on which had been scrawled in ink, *To Dad* **LOVE** Alex. The word, **LOVE**, printed in large block letters, almost dominated an entire side of the stitched, white, leather sphere.

"That is the ball he gave me after his first pitching victory. He told me that I deserved it for all the hours I worked with him. I saw that game, and I remember the score as if it all happened this morning. Our team won, eight to one, and Alex allowed only three hits. I had that baseball in my suitcase, when my life fell apart, otherwise I'd have nothing . . ."

The tree shadows were merging into blue twilight, and a soft mist was floating above the pond by the time the old man walked me slowly to my car. Suddenly, he halted, touched my arm gently and asked, "Mark, are you familiar with the Century Plant that grows in the southwest?"

"Sure, we saw plenty of them when we were in Arizona in January. Lovely things with clusters of swordlike, jagged, blue leaves, all growing out of a small base."

"Exactly. It's called the Century Plant because it's supposed to live at least a hundred years, but it rarely does. It grows rather slowly for perhaps ten or twenty or even fifty years until one day, with no advance warning, it suddenly sends up a thick stalk from its center, a stalk that may grow as high as twenty feet in less than a month. Then the top of the stalk erupts into hundreds of sprays of tiny yellow flowers for a week or more, high above every other living thing in the desert."

It was almost dark, but I could feel the old man staring at me. His grip on my arm grew firmer. "Do you know what happens next, Mark?"

"No, I don't."

"The flowers are blown away by the wind, the tall stalk dries up quickly and crashes to the ground, and the Century Plant after its all too brief, single moment of glory, shrivels up and dies, a sad but accurate metaphor for many of us who achieve great success. Movie stars, writers, sports figures, even politicians—people who burst on the world scene almost overnight and tumble to the ground just as swiftly. I was a Century Plant, Mark, and I have spent more than half my life now trying to convince myself that, like the real plant, I had no control over my destiny."

It seemed like a long ride home. Two questions kept turning over in my mind. Why had he really asked me to visit him, and why had he bothered to tell me about the Century Plant?

I slept very little, that night.

XVII

EARLY ON THE MORNING OF AUGUST 10, AFTER A SLEEPY ride from Jaffrey, I parted company with my family at Logan Airport in East Boston. After many hugs and kisses, plus a few tears, the three of them moved closer to each other as I picked up my attaché case and flight bag and stepped into the jetway leading to the plane's entrance. I thought I heard Louise call my name. I stopped and looked back. Todd and Glenn each had an arm around their mother, and all three were waving and shouting, "Break a leg, break a leg!" I almost cancelled the tour, right there.

Goliath's Books' publicity department had mapped out my trip with all the precision and timing of a space launch. Flying to Seattle, my first scheduled stop, I reviewed once more the contents of a hefty blue notebook they had supplied me that contained not only twenty-six airline tickets but my daily itinerary for each of the forty-eight days including New York. Beginning on the West Coast, and working my way east, the promotion routing had been arranged with a minimum of backtracking. Following Seattle I would appear next in Portland, then San Francisco, Los Angeles, San Diego, across to Phoenix, north to Salt Lake City, east to Denver, south to Albuquerque, and then down into Dallas-Fort Worth and Houston and on across the nation to sixteen other cities ending in New York City on September 27 and 28. In city after city I had excellent interviewers, kindly and perceptive for the most part, asking questions about life and success and methods of coping in a world so obsessed with material things. There were also a few who did their best to make me out a fool, a rich fool they were quick to point out, or a hustler who had written a book not to help humanity but to make a lot of bucks. I tried, while controlling my temper, to answer them, but soon discovered that it was unnecessary, especially on the phone-in programs. Whenever I was attacked by the hosts of those shows, my unseen but very vocal public always rose to my defense and ripped away, in call after call, at my inhospitable questioner. Most of all I remember the faces in the stores, faces filled with hope and determination that they would make it, faces watching my hands with reverence and awe as I inscribed copies of *A Better Way to Live* for them or a loved one.

During the first two weeks I lost twelve pounds, and although the days began to get longer and longer as my energy level sank, I was still sustained every evening by my phone call back to Louise and the boys. No matter how late I returned to my room, after my final appearance of the day or night, I always made contact with my family.

Halfway through the tour, I called home one evening from St. Louis. Louise answered, and I could sense more than the usual amount of excitement in her voice. "Mark, Todd has some great news to tell you, and he's been doing the fidgets all evening, waiting for your call. Here, I'll let him tell you, himself."

"Dad?"

"Yes, son."

"Remember what I told you, a couple of months ago, when you were working with me in the yard, teaching me how to pitch?"

My weary mind couldn't. "Gee, Todd, we talked about so many things. Help me a little."

"Remember I told you that I would pitch a no-hit game for you this year?"

"Don't tell me—"

"I did it, Dad! I did it! Today! No hits and no runs and I only walked three!"

"Wow! That's sensational. Congratulations, son! I'm so proud of you. You've made my day, and you've made my trip, with that news. I'm so sorry I couldn't have been there, but thank you, thank you! I miss you very much."

"I miss you too, Dad. We'll see you soon. Here's Mom again."

I waited. Louise didn't come back on the line immediately.

"Louise? Louise, are you there?"

"I'm here, hon. I just wanted to wait until Todd was out of range. Something I've got to tell you . . ."

"What? What happened?"

"Well, after the last out, today, Coach Murphy awarded Todd the game ball. And all the way home he sat next to me in the front seat, with the ball in his glove, saying nothing. Finally, I asked him why he looked so sad after pitching such a super game, and he began to cry and said it didn't really mean that much because his dad didn't see it."

"Oh, God . . ."

"Do you know what's sitting on your dresser, tonight?"

"What?"

"A baseball. The game ball. He autographed it when he got home. It says, *'To Dad,* **LOVE***, Todd'* and the word **'LOVE'** is printed in large, fat letters!"

XVIII

THE TWO PROMOTIONAL DAYS IN MEMPHIS HAD BEEN EX-
citing and productive. At least nine, on a scale of one to
ten. Great interviews and enthusiastic crowds storming
the bookstores plus a phone call from David Coronet, on
my first day in that lovely city, informing me that as
closely as his sales department and their computers could
track things, we had sold more than seven million paperback copies of our book in five weeks, a publishing
record. Another piece of good news that he knew would
please me, he said, was that *A Better Way to Live* had now
reached the top of the paperback bestseller list, according
to *Publishers Weekly*, while sales of the hardcover edition
kept it still perched atop the hardcover list—a feat no
book had ever accomplished before.

After hugging Goliath Books' Memphis representative,
Marcia Bechtol, and thanking her for being such a perfect
guardian angel to me for forty-eight hours, I boarded

Delta's flight 1774 slightly after nine in the evening. Arrival time in Atlanta, next leg of my journey, was 11:26 P.M., including the hour difference in time, but the tightly packed schedule of each day no longer bothered me. I had actually become accustomed to the routine, spurred on now by the knowledge that after Atlanta there would only be seven more cities to visit, two weeks to go, before I would be reunited with my family.

"Looks as if we're going to have you all to ourselves, sir," the smiling flight attendant remarked as she took my jacket and glanced around the empty first class cabin area. "May I get you something before we take off?"

I shook my head, grateful that she had not recognized me. After five autograph sessions in Memphis, that day, I had just about exhausted my supply of small talk.

I must have dozed off as soon as my head touched the backrest only to be awakened by the plane's lurching motions as it taxied out to its takeoff position. Someone was now occupying the seat next to me. Someone indeed! Alexander Anthony carefully tucked his white suede jacket beneath his safety belt before he turned and extended his large hand toward me. "Mark, it's good to see you again so soon. You are looking well. The tour seems to have agreed with you."

What could I say? He was the last person I expected to meet on a night flight to Atlanta. Or anywhere else. While I was struggling to focus my thoughts, the 727 suddenly lunged forward, accelerating down the runway with a roar of straining horsepower and creaks and groans and bumps, and soon we were airborne, banking immediately to the right. Speechless, I continued to blink at the old man until he grinned and patted my knee as if I were a child. "I hope that you don't mind my sitting next to you, especially since we both have rather long legs. You must be very tired after the day you've had, and with all these empty seats up here I'm sure they will allow me to move so that you can stretch out and nap."

"Mind?" I asked limply. "Of course I don't mind, Alex. It's wonderful to see you again. I'm just trying to recover from the shock of waking up and finding you, of all people, sitting next to me. What were you doing in Memphis? Visiting friends? I thought you told me that no one knows who you are, or do you travel incognito?"

He chuckled. "Incognito? Yes, yes. Sometimes I do have to resort to that in these odd jobs that are assigned to me. As a matter of fact I'm flying with you now in the line of duty."

I shook my head. At least I could humor the old man. "And I suppose you're using another name on this assignment?"

He nodded.

"Mind telling me what it is?"

"Salom," he said softly. "A. B. Salom."

In the dim lights of the cabin I could see those pale blue eyes studying my face, trying to read my reaction to his words. My heart was pounding as I unbuckled my safety belt and uncrossed my legs.

"You?" I cried in a voice I didn't even recognize as mine. "You!"

He said nothing.

"You're the crackpot who has been sending us those cutesy messages in calligraphy that have caused us so much anguish? And you're not Alexander Anthony?"

"Mark, I *am* Alexander Anthony. With those notes I was merely trying to warn you in advance of what was to come, and I reasoned that you would be perceptive enough to interpret their meaning, especially if I signed them A. B. Salom."

Now I was struggling to control my temper. "What meaning? Please, I'm lousy at riddles!"

"Absalom. The son of David. His death in battle and his father's reaction to that tragic ending. David crying out, 'My son, my son . . . would I had died for thee.' "

"Alex, I don't understand what the hell you're driving at. And I refuse to believe that anyone with your intelligence would resort to such a sick pastime. You can't be the sender of those weird messages."

The old man sighed, shrugged his shoulders, reached forward and removed Delta's inflight magazine, SKY, from the pocket of the seat in front of him. He withdrew a giant fountain pen from his inside jacket pocket, removed its cap slowly, wrote on the magazine's cover and handed it to me. My stomach flip-flopped. There was my name inscribed in the same delicate blue calligraphy that had haunted us on all three notes we had received. Suddenly I felt the same sensation I always get in a dentist's chair. That helpless, trapped feeling—powerless—all control abandoned to another. But I couldn't surrender without a struggle.

"Alex, that invitation of yours to visit you in Stoddard?"

"Yes?"

"Why didn't you use the same notepaper and envelope as the other notes you sent, and why didn't you write to me in calligraphy and sign the thing as you did the others, A. B. Salom?"

He shook his head. "Because if I had, Mark, you would have contacted your friend at the Federal Bureau of Investigation in Boston. He would have insisted on accompanying you to see me, and that would have complicated matters."

"How . . . how could you possibly know about him? Only Louise . . ."

"Son, don't fight me. I do know. Accept it. I wanted you to visit me alone, in Stoddard, because I had a very important message I was entrusted to deliver to you. Those are the odd jobs I perform, now and then. I am simply a messenger. But the longer we were together, that day, the more fond I became of you, until I could not find it in my heart to fulfill my unpleasant duty. It is the first assignment that I have ever botched."

As much as I wanted to hear that message, I still had to test him. "Alex, how many notes did you send?"

"Three."

"How did you deliver the first?"

"I dropped it in a mailbag that was delivered to your house, in Jaffrey, along with other mailbags."

"And no one saw you?"

"No one sees me, unless I want them to see me."

"The second note?"

"It was left at the desk for you, at the Arizona Biltmore in Phoenix. I almost missed you with that one."

"The third?"

"I placed it in your room at the New York Hilton, along with a basket of excellent fruit."

"You were in the ballroom at the Hilton, that night? You heard me speak?"

"A lovely homage to your departed mother. Yes, I heard you."

"Well, if you were so close to me in Jaffrey and Phoenix and New York, why did you bother with written messages? Why didn't you just come up to me and speak your piece?"

"Because it was not yet time. There is a schedule for all things. The notes were my idea, and I have already been chastised for sending them. But I had hoped they would open your mind, prepare you in some small way, especially if you picked up on the Absalom theme regarding father and son."

"My wife came close. But I still don't understand. What is it that I was supposed to be thinking about? I'm very tired, Alex, and I'm not so sure that we shouldn't have the police waiting for you with a straitjacket when we land in Atlanta."

He drained his coffee cup, squashed the styrofoam container in his huge fist, and placed the smashed remains in the pocket of the seat in front.

"Mark, believe me, I beg of you. I am not a lunatic, and this is not a game. I merely have a message for you. I deliver several each year. I faltered when you were at my home in Stoddard, but this time I will not fail."

"Okay, let me have it."

"Son," he said haltingly, "I know how much you love your family. It is my sad duty to inform you that one of them will not live out this year."

I was having difficulty breathing. "How . . . how in God's name do you know that?"

"Exactly."

"What?"

"I know it because this message is in God's name."

"Alex, Alex," I groaned. "Do you expect me to believe that you're some kind of an angel and that you're delivering a message from above? I'm afraid you've lived alone, with all your thoughts and regrets, too long. I think you need help. When we get to Atlanta why don't I see what I can do . . ."

"Mark, dear friend, I forfeited all need for help a long time ago. You must believe, you must accept my message as fact."

"Someone in my family is about to die?"

"Before the first day of the New Year. It has already been posted above," he replied, pointing over his head.

I closed my eyes, debating whether or not to ring for the flight attendant. Decided against it. Might as well play along. "Okay, who?"

"Your younger son, Todd."

I stared out the small window at the cloudless blue night. A full moon reflected brightly off the taut aluminum wing just outside. Without turning to face him, I asked, "Is it known how my son will die?"

"It is known, of course," he sighed, "but not by me. All I can do is pass on what I have been instructed to transmit."

"Alex," I said, "people die every second of the day and night, all over the world. And certainly without any advance notice from our friend upstairs. Why bother to go through all this trouble with me?"

"Because you are a very special person, Mark. You have transformed millions of lives with your book, and this world is a much better place because of your efforts. Great credit has been accumulated by you, in the eyes of God, and you are entitled to special consideration. You have been granted a rare option, a choice that only you can exercise, and that is what I was trying to prepare you for in my crude notes."

"An option?"

"Mark, because you are so special, it has been decided that you can prevent your son's death, if you wish."

"If I wish? I would do anything to save my son. Any father would."

He patted my hand. "You are not any father. The countless lives you have already rescued place you in a rare and unique category."

"Okay, so what must I do to save my son?"

He continued to pat my hand. "I'm afraid there is only one way. You can save him provided you agree to take his place on the schedule. This is a very unusual dispensation, granted to a select few each year, only those who are looked upon with special favor and grace."

I tried to force a smile. "Some choice!"

He frowned at me. "It was believed that because of your deep love for your son you would be grateful for this option."

"Alex, how do I know that you are what you claim to be?"

He raised both hands, palms upward. "I regret that I cannot show you an identification card signed by God. I have no proof that what I say is any more than the rantings of an old man with a warped mind and a macabre sense of humor. That is always the greatest challenge in this job. But you will know, you will know . . ."

"And when am I supposed to make this choice?"

"Had I delivered my message when I was scheduled to, on the day you visited my home in Stoddard, you would have had more time to ponder this terrible dilemma, and for that I am deeply sorry. But now I'm afraid you have very little time remaining, which is why it was necessary for me to meet with you, alone, on this flight. Your decision must be reached by midnight on September 28."

My nervous laughter was hollow and short-lived. September 28, of all nights. The climax to my triumphant tour. The night I would speak to a packed house at Yankee Stadium plus an audience of countless millions on television. Fourteen days from today!

"And how do I announce my decision, my choice? Will you be visiting me on that day?"

"No, no, I'm afraid we'll not see each other again, at least in the near future. As I understand your schedule, you will be speaking in Yankee Stadium on the twenty-eighth, sometime after ten o'clock."

"At ten-thirty."

"The method you are to employ to announce your decision is a simple one. If you have decided that your son should live and that you will take his place by abdicating your own life, you are to wear a red necktie that evening when you deliver your speech. Your response will be noted and acted upon, either way. Please find it in your heart to forgive me. I cannot tell you how it grieves me to be the bearer of such awesome news, and I have long ago ceased questioning the logic behind my messages. I volunteered to be the one to tell you because, as a fellow writer, I thought that perhaps I might be able to soften the blow a little."

Tears were now streaming down his wrinkled cheeks. I reached across and held his hand. "And after September 28, how long will it be before . . . before? . . ."

He shrugged his shoulders. "I don't know, Mark. Certainly no later than the first day of the new year."

I could feel myself perspiring despite the jets of cool air that were blowing down from above. Was this really happening to me? Or was this all a crazy dream? Alex unbuckled his seat belt, rose, and strode slowly toward the lavatory. I clenched my fists and stared out the window at the tiny bobbing lights on the distant wing tip.

"Sir, will you please fasten your seat belt. We'll be landing shortly."

"Landing? We only took off ten or fifteen minutes ago."

She looked at me strangely. "We've been in the air almost an hour, Mr. Christopher. Please fasten your belt."

I nodded toward the empty seat next to me. "My friend is still in the lavatory. Maybe I should check to see if he's okay."

"Who, sir?"

"My friend, Mr. Anthony—er-r-r Salom. The man who was sitting next to me."

Her smile vanished instantly. "Sir, there has been no one sitting next to you. You've been solo all the way—the only passenger up front here."

"What are you talking about? He's been sitting right here since we left Memphis."

She backed away. "Mr. Christopher, there has been no other passenger up here."

She was wrong. I knew she was wrong. I reached into the back pocket of the seat in front of where Alex had sat, groping for the crushed coffee cup he had placed there. Nothing. The attendant handed me her clipboard.

"As you can see, sir, I entered only one name in this first class seating plan. Mark Christopher. No one else."

"Have I been sleeping?"

"No. I offered you a pillow, but you refused. We even talked about your book for quite a while, don't you remember?"

Without answering I unbuckled my seat belt, stepped out into the aisle, and ran the few steps toward the lavatory that Alex had entered. The tiny illuminated window on the door read "Vacant." I jerked open the door and stared inside. Vacant!

"Will you please return to your seat, sir," the young lady said firmly as she glanced toward the back of the plane. Meekly, I did as I was told, buckled my seat belt, and sat slumped in my seat as we circled Atlanta International Airport preparatory to landing. As I turned to look out the window again, my foot slipped on the magazine I had dropped earlier. I reached down and retrieved it.

Beneath the magazine's bright red title, SKY, was my name, written in that familiar calligraphy! And then, for the first time, I noticed the illustration on the cover. Against a purple background of somber mountains and bleached desert sand stood a single, large Century Plant, its uppermost jagged blue leaf pointing directly at my name.

XIX

HANDS ON HIPS, DAVID CORONET STOOD AT THE WINDOW of my suite at the New York Hilton, scowling through the rain-streaked window at the glistening traffic far below on the Avenue of the Americas.

"Damn, damn!" he cursed, bobbing his head furiously. From my room phone he had just canceled the ticker-tape parade that Goliath had planned for me, up Broadway, after talking at length with the National Weather Service.

"They told me I should be counting my blessings," he growled, "because there's a much bigger tropical storm headed up this way that could become a hurricane in a few days, named Ernesto. Hell of a name for a storm. Thought they always gave them women's names."

"They did," I said, "until three years ago. This equal rights stuff works both ways, you know."

"Well, we're not licked yet," he grumbled as he checked his watch. "The weather boys told me that the eye of the storm has turned out to sea, near Cape Lookout, and this miserable rain should end by the middle of the afternoon so our Yankee Stadium bash is still on, thank God. I'd hate to think of the problems we'd have trying to refund more than sixty thousand tickets if we couldn't reschedule this. How about Louise? Is she coming in to see her hero capture the big city?"

"Impossible. She phoned from Logan about an hour ago. They're socked in good, up there, and expect to be for several hours. She's on her way back home to watch it all on television."

"A shame. This is a proud night . . . for her, too."

"She'll be with our boys, and they can all sweat me out together."

He lit another cigar. "I've had so much on my mind, Mark, that I forgot to tell you. You were just great, yesterday, on the *Today Show*."

"Jane Pauley made it easy for me."

"I missed you, today, on *Good Morning, America*. How did that go?"

"David Hartman kept plugging our televised speech tonight on ABC."

"Good, good."

He glanced at his watch again. "Now, what's your schedule for the rest of the day?"

"Stuart will pick me up at one. We're autographing for an hour at Macy's and an hour at Doubleday's, and then I'm coming back here to take a nap. Lately, I've been running out of gas in the middle of the afternoon."

"Yes, yes, by all means rest. You've had a horrendous schedule, and we're all so grateful for the magnificent job you did everywhere. The program at the stadium is scheduled to commence at nine. Dr. Peale will deliver the invocation, and then we've got three of the finest motivational speakers in the country lined up, Cavett Robert, Charles 'Tremendous' Jones, and Charles Jarvis. They'll each do about twenty minutes of positive, upbeat stuff."

"I've heard them all. You've made it very difficult for me, Dave. I don't know how you expect me to follow those three pros."

He waved his cigar. "Not to worry. You'll be terrific. Now, when should I pick you up to go to the ballpark? Do you want to hear the other speakers?"

"If you don't mind, Dave, I'd rather stay here as long as possible and conserve my energy."

"No problem," he said, checking his watch once more. "Tell you what. I'll come up here to your room at nine. That'll give us plenty of time to get uptown in the traffic, okay?"

After he was gone I opened my attaché case and removed the file cards on which I had printed the notes for my speech. Each was numbered, in the upper right-hand corner, and I found myself gazing at card number eight before I realized that I had not actually read a single word. I stared out the window at the falling rain, thinking how swiftly the two weeks had flown since that memorable plane ride from Memphis. As hard as I concentrated, I found it difficult to recall very many of the details of my ensuing visits to Cleveland, Pittsburgh, Washington, D.C., Baltimore, Philadelphia, and Boston—except for my lunch with the President and First Lady at the White House and the two days that Louise had spent with me during my Boston visit.

I had agonized for days on whether I should tell Louise about my second meeting with Alexander Anthony, finally deciding that it would serve no purpose by tormenting her other than shifting some of the heavy load of anguish from my shoulders to hers. Loving us as she did, how could she possibly even think about making a choice between her son and her husband? What wife and mother could? No, the ultimate decision would be mine alone, and once I had accepted that chilling fact I was able to conceal my terrible problem, even as perceptive as she is, so that we enjoyed our forty-eight hours together in Boston during the little free time we had between my interviews and autographing sessions.

Stuart picked me up, on schedule, at one. I signed books, nonstop, at both Macy's and Doubleday's and was back in my room by four. I napped until my alarm began whining, precisely at six, ordered an egg salad sandwich and milk from room service, showered and shaved. Then, after nibbling on half the sandwich and downing the milk, I propped myself up in bed, wearing only my shorts, and tried to concentrate on my file card notes.

An hour later I was still struggling. What was wrong with me? The words I had rehearsed so many times during the past several weeks, powerful phrases proclaiming the most positive and constructive principles from my book, now seemed weak and ineffectual when I spoke them aloud. I tried again, from the beginning. No better. Sounded more like a bored high school student delivering a book report. I knew it wasn't the material. It was me. I had no heart for this evening's circus, and the words into which I was trying to breathe life sounded bland and inadequate because I had repeated them, in interview after interview, until I now felt more like a parrot than an ambassador of success.

There was still an hour before I had to start dressing. Was that time enough to put together another and better speech? Maybe. I leaped from my bed, removed a stack of blank file cards from my case, and sat at the small octagon table near the window. Twenty minutes later I heaved my pen against the far wall. Despair. I had printed just one word on a single card—*Absalom*! The subconscious had become conscious. The truth had finally surfaced, and I had to face it. This was the night Mark Christopher had to make the most important choice of his life . . . Todd or me . . . blue tie or red tie.

I flung myself back on the bed, feeling both light-headed and nauseous. How could I face that huge crowd, and the television cameras, with charm and gusto and enthusiasm when my heart was bursting? How? Even though my head was partially buried in the soft pillow, I could still see the gold-framed picture of Louise and Todd and Glenn that I had placed on every night table, in every hotel, in every city. I could picture them soon, in our living room, sitting together, nervously waiting for the big moment when their father and husband appeared on their television screen. How could I let them down with a mediocre performance? And if I did, I could visualize tomorrow's headlines—"Mr. Success strikes out in Yankee Stadium!" Oh God, God!

God?

A Bible lay on the night table, next to the picture. I sat up and took it in my hands. When I was a kid, my mother and I had our own special game that we often played in the evening before she tucked me in. We would each open her Bible, at random, place our finger on whatever page faced us, and read aloud the verse we were touching. That, she had always assured me, was our own very special message from God to help us deal with the problems of the moment. I believed her. Well, I had already received one message recently, courtesy of Alexander Anthony. Why not another?

I let the Bible fall open in my hands and ran my finger down the right-hand page with my eyes closed.

When I looked, my forefinger was resting on two verses from Matthew:

But when they deliver you up, take no thought how or what ye shall speak: for it shall be given you in that same hour what ye shall speak.

For it is not ye that speak, but the Spirit of your Father which speaketh in you.

I closed the Bible gently, feeling more at peace with myself than I had in two weeks.

At ten-fifteen, David Coronet led me through the spacious New York Yankee locker room and into the crowded dugout where I shook hands with Dr. Peale and the three speakers who all wished me luck. A huge platform had been erected behind home plate and thousands of folding chairs, all occupied, covered the infield. Far out in centerfield I could see a quarter-size replica of the Tower of Success around which a marching band was performing. The stands were packed, and the crowd had already begun a rhythmic chant, "Mr. Success, Mr. Success, we want Mr. Success!" How many times, from this very same plot of land, had similar cries gone up for Ruth and Gehrig and DiMaggio and Mantle and Maris? I felt numb and fought back the urge to flee. To hide. Anywhere!

A hand gripped my right elbow. David pointed toward the three television cameras on tripods, one positioned on each foul line with the third resting on a low pedestal out where I figured the pitcher's mound was located.

"That little guy wearing the golf cap, next to the third base camera," David shouted in my ear, "he's our program director. When he cues me by pointing in this direction, I'll walk on out, climb the platform steps, go over to the mike, and introduce you. Now, when you hear me say, 'Let's hear it for Mr. Success!' you come out slowly. Take your time going up the steps. Milk it. Let the applause build until they blow the grandstand roof off this place. Got it?"

I nodded.

"Where are your notes?" he yelled.

"I have none."

"Wow! You're going to wing it for twenty-three minutes?"

"Not exactly."

I could barely hear him above the clamor. "Not exactly? What does that mean?"

Just then we saw the little man in the golf cap pointing toward us.

"I hope you know what you're doing, guy," David cried. "Good luck!"

"Thanks," I said, clearing my throat and reaching for a handkerchief to wipe the nervous perspiration from my face. "God," I whispered, "please help me now!"

"Oh, by the way, you look great, Mark," David yelled over his shoulder as he headed for the platform. "Love that suit. Elegant. Looks magnificent with that red tie!"

XX

I HAVE ABSOLUTELY NO RECOLLECTION AT ALL OF DELIVering a speech. I do remember approaching the flag-draped podium with its battery of microphones and acknowledging the thunderous applause with nervous waves and smiles.

I can also remember bowing and tossing kisses to the bobbing ocean of smiling faces at the finish, during what David later told me exultantly was a twenty-minute, standing ovation. Of the speech itself, nothing. Zero recall! Not even when Louise replayed it for me on our home video recorder was I able to recognize a single phrase I had uttered.

Five days after my Yankee Stadium appearance, on Sunday, October 3, Goliath Books ran full page ads in thirty of the major newspapers in the United States, reprinting the speech verbatim, except for my opening greetings to the people and my thanks to David Coronet for his magnificent introduction.

A copy of the speech, from one of the advertisements, follows . . .

THE KEY TO A BETTER LIFE

Man or woman . . . wherever these words have found you, turn away from your travail and struggles of the hour and give me your hand. Come with me on a mission of exploration, a journey of the mind that may help you to change your life for the better.

We are not, you and I, searching for gold or silver or oil but for something far more valuable—a key—a simple key that will unlock our prison door and free us from our hell of unhappiness, insecurity, and failure so that we can at least have the opportunity to fulfill our dreams. That same key, if we find it, will unlock the greatest puzzle box of humanity and unveil the answer to a question that has haunted and occupied most of man-kind for centuries . . .

Is there a better way to live?

We have been told that man is the only animal that knows nothing, and can learn nothing without being taught. He can neither speak nor walk nor eat nor do anything at the prompting of nature except weep.

During the rush of centuries we have been taught many things, but our weeping did not diminish as our knowledge increased. Tears of despondency, failure, frustration, self-pity, helplessness and fear are as common today as when Homer cried that among all creatures that breathe on earth and crawl on it there is not anywhere a thing more dismal than man.

Why is this so? Why are we unhappy? Have we not been told that we were created in the image of God, and did we not receive complete dominion over this world? When did we reject our image? How did we abdicate our power? What went wrong? Why do we feel, in our hearts, that we are as unfulfilled today as were our ancestors whose every waking moment was spent in struggles merely to survive?

Did God abandon us somewhere along the way? Did He grow weary of our failure to take full advantage of the minds and the talents He breathed into us, and the paradise He willed us, and move on to other worlds, other galaxies, leaving us to fend for ourselves? Would He, in his infinite knowledge, do such a thing after building so many contradictions into each of us that He certainly must have forseen that trouble was inevitable?

Man is the only animal that blushes and laughs, and yet this same creature, who can be so tender and loving, is the only living thing that constantly preys on its own species. Why? Why does he kill, steal, rape, pillage, lie, and cheat if he is, in truth, the pinnacle of creation? Why does he, through his foolish actions, condemn himself to a life of servitude, misery, failure, and frustration if he is the center of the cosmos and the recipient of so many blessings from God? And—if we have been living in this sorry state for so many millenia, is there any reason to believe that we can change now, that we can discover a better way to live?

That is what our quest is all about, yours and mine, so hear me out and hear me well. What we can accomplish together may well determine how you will spend the rest of your days.

Let us embark on this journey, as all journeys

should begin, with a clear understanding of where we are when we start out. Your response to five questions should accurately fix your position, your present location on life's winding road:

Are you in control of your life?

Are you at peace with yourself and those around you?

Are you proud of your life's accomplishments?

Are you and your family enjoying the fruits of your work?

Are you happy and contented?

Simple questions, yes. But difficult to answer. Painful. Painful because those who can reply to all five in the affirmative, truthfully, are as rare as a twenty-carat flawless diamond. Gather these fortunate people together, from the four corners of our earth, and you would see that they are only a minute percentage of our six billion inhabitants.

Why? Why can we not live in peace and tranquility and pride and contentment and happiness on a bountiful sphere that was willed to us with love?

Are we merely puppets—actors and actresses on a stage—following scripts of prophecies made by anguished wise men of the past? Was Job correct when he cried, "Man that is born of woman is of few days and full of trouble"? Was Sophocles bemoaning our true fate when he asked, "What trouble is beyond the range of man? What heavy burden will he not endure?" or Lucretius when he dipped his reed in ink and wrote, "O miserable minds of men! O blinded beasts! In what darkness of life and in how great dangers is passed this term of life whatever its duration!"

It is an easy game to mock man's efforts to live a

better life since he was banished from Eden. Huge followings have been attracted by those who scornfully declare that all mortals are fools and that we are all born with halters around our neck. Their words, echoing through our history and literature, provide an easy refuge and excuse for us when we fail, when we finally grow weary of trying to improve our conditions, when we have been struck down by forces beyond our control, when a succession of setbacks has drained our resources. Defeat, somehow, seems easier to bear knowing that this was the fate prophesied for us by so many men of genius. Thus we allow ourselves to drown in a sea of mediocrity after little struggle, or we allow our true potential to rust because of disuse, or we wander through what could have been the best years of our lives filled with bitterness and self-pity and catch only an occasional fleeting glimpse of what might have been. Prophecy fulfilled.

Why have we allowed this tragedy, this plague of failure and unhappiness, to infect us? Why are we able to conquer dreaded diseases, circle distant planets, view events thousands of miles away from the comfort of our homes, design machines that can tend to our every wish, transplant our own organs, even create life in a test tube and yet make so little progress in elevating man's opinion of himself and his many talents?

Are the prophets of doom, both past and present, correct? Are we here for no purpose? Is this world, this spinning ball that we inhabit, not much other than an anthill, where some ants carry corn, and some carry their young, and some go empty, and all go to and fro on a little heap of dust? Is our life, our most valuable possession, no more than a little gleam of time between two eternities with no second chance for us, ever?

Why is it that in the most prosperous and vital nation that ever existed, more than three hundred thousand individuals attempt to end their lives each year? Why is it that we are so unable to cope with the realities of our days that more than fifty million prescriptions for Valium were dispensed in this country last year? Why are we forced to treat more than four thousand new mental cases every twenty-four hours and stand by helplessly while the number of heroin addicts and cocaine addicts and alcoholics rises to epidemic proportions? Is this how we must live, dreading the failures and horrors of each day with so much passion that we are willing to escape even if our flight destroys us?

There must be a better way to live.

There is a better way to live!

When we were given dominion over the world, we were also given dominion over ourselves. God is not our navigator. It was never His intention to chart a course for each of us and thus place us all under His bondage. Instead, He bestowed each of us with intellect and talent and vision to map our own way, to write our own Book of Life in any manner that we choose.

Choice! The key is choice. You have options. You need not spend your life wallowing in failure, ignorance, grief, poverty, shame, and self-pity. But, hold on! If this is true, then why have so many among us apparently elected to live in that manner? Who would be fool enough to choose failure over success, ignorance over knowledge, poverty over wealth? No one! So how do we explain that vast multitude of humanity that continues to exist in hopeless mediocrity, unfulfilled, frustrated, envious, drained of confidence and self-esteem, unable to meet even their daily obligations and sad—so sad that each new day produces no fresh seedling of hope, only more weeds of despair from showers of tears?

The answer is simple and obvious. Those who live in unhappy failure have never exercised their options for the better things of life because they have never been aware that they had any choices! Life to them has never beem a game of skill where study and hard work and courage and perseverance can be brought into play to turn failure into success, misery into happiness. Instead, these vast legions of losers look upon life as a war where they are always on the defensive, struggling with their own inferior talents against superior forces—a war they are always doomed to lose because they have come to believe that the only choice they have is to survive, or perish. How sad!

If you know what it is to eat the crumbs of failure, to labor drudgingly with only unhappiness as your constant companion, to sleep with tears of despair and hopelessness, let the dark curtain be pulled back for you. Look closely. Consider the choices still available to you, choices that you can elect immediately, no matter what your present condition may be, so that you can live the remainder of your life as your creator intended for you to live—in glory, not in shame.

Adopt the words that follow as your words. Clutch them to your heart and let these old principles, these forgotten rules, these sacred canons of the past, all become a public declaration of your intention to live a better life. This is your personal manifesto . . .

So many of us awake each morning with dread in our heart. To face the monotony of another day with its ceaseless toil and pressures for so little reward is agony. We bathe, we put on our costume and reluctantly force

*ourselves to crawl from our cocoon to confront a world
we imagine is ready to devour us or trample us underfoot.
Each day repeats the drudgery of the last, except that the
hours seem to grow painfully longer as the years pass.
The body is weary. The mind is numb. The obligations
increase. The future is dim. Finally, the day ends. Blessed
sleep. Oblivion. And then the sun rises again.*

I choose a better way to live!

Henceforth, each morning, I will awake and fall
to my knees and give thanks to God for the gift that
only He can bestow—a new day. This is my most
priceless possession. If ever I should feel ungrateful
and treat this miracle lightly, I need only open my
morning newspaper to the obituary page and scan
the long list of names there—names of people who
would be most pleased to change places with me
despite my problems. There are no problems in a
cemetery. I would rather be here than there. I am
grateful for this fresh opportunity. I will show my
gratitude in everything I do, this day. A sundial
counts only the hours of sunshine, but I will count
them all. I will treasure each minute. I am immortal
until my work is done and I have only begun. Thank
you for these new hours, God. I needed this day to
prove that your faith in my ability was not misplaced.
I depart from home smiling. The birds—when did I
last hear them singing? How fortunate I am to be
here.

*So many of us spend our lives searching for happiness.
Like children hunting Easter eggs, we dash hither and yon
hoping to discover some mystical bluebird. Life would be*

so different, we sigh, if only we were happy. And so, one hurries home to be happy and another flees home to be happy. One is getting married to be happy and another is getting divorced to be happy. One takes expensive cruises to be happy and another labors overtime to be happy. Endless search. Wasted years. Madness. Always the moon is out of reach, the fruit not quite ripe, the wine too dry. Shadows. Tears. Our pillow knows the truth.

I choose a better way to live!

Henceforth, my pursuit of happiness has ended. How blind I have been! Now I know that happiness hides not in that new house, that new career, that new friend. And it is never for sale. When I cannot find contentment in myself, it is useless to seek it elsewhere. Whenever I depend on things outside myself to supply me with joy I am doomed to disappointment. Happiness, I see now, has nothing to do with getting. It consists of being satisfied with what I've got and what I haven't got. Few things are necessary to make the wise man happy while no amount of material wealth would satisfy a fool. I am not a fool. I have drawn a circle around me. Whenever I reach across it I will be giving, not taking. My needs are few. So long as I have something to do, someone to love, and something to hope for, I shall be happy. Now I know that the only source of happiness is within me, and I will begin to share it. Like a perfume, I know that I cannot pour it on others without getting a few drops on myself.

So many of us count the hours of our work as slavery. We limp through each day as if there were irons on our legs, our hands reluctantly on the task at hand, our eyes always on the clock. Let this day pass, we pray, so that we can escape from this abominable place into the darkness. We flinch at the voice of authority, despising the power that decrees how we should act, how we must think on the job. We feel so helpless. Like a child. Disobey and we will be punished. Our food, our shelter, our very existence ordains that we must labor. Is this our total fate? Are these tools, this sales talk, this lifeless computer, my entire future until death frees me? Is this all there is? Let me rest.

I choose a better way to live!

Henceforth, I will deal with any chore that confronts me, no matter how menial, no matter how arduous, no matter how boring, as if my entrance into heaven depended on it being completed to the best of my ability. Now I know the most certain secret of success ever shared with man. Now I know that if I always do more than is expected of me, in all I'm asked to do, I cannot help but take long strides toward a better and more fulfilling career. My task of the moment is not a life sentence. I have the key to free myself. All I need do is throw myself into my work with enthusiasm, with initiative, and with love, and the shackles will fall from my legs. I am not a cog. I am the wheel and I must prove it. How? By demonstrating with action that I am far more valuable than the coins I now receive. This job of the moment is only a way station. God has bigger plans for me, but they will never be achieved by accident. I must earn the privilege of dealing with greater challenges. I can grow, right here, right now, with whatever is at hand to do. My reward will come. I have faith.

So many of us think ourselves into smallness, into inferiority, by thinking downward. We are held back by too much caution. We are timid about venturing. We are not bold enough. And so we die before we reach middle age, although we will not be lowered into the ground until we pass three score and ten. What happened to the grand dreams of our youth? Suicide. Struck down by our own caution, our own lack of faith in ourselves and our abilities. Opportunities? There were many. But always there was risk. Do we dare? We vaccillate. Time hurries by. Opportunity gone. We anguish. The years roll on. Finally, we convince ourselves that it's too late and settle for cheap imitations of life. We envy the achievers. How lucky they are.

I choose a better way to live!

Henceforth, I will take every risk and embrace every opportunity that may provide a better life for me and my family. I no longer believe that a rolling stone gathers no moss. Better to be in motion, even if the energy is wasted, than buried forever in a shady plot. That will come soon enough. I will despise myself later if I look back on my life and realize that I had the talent and the ability to do great things but could not find the courage to try. I know what I can do, and I know how little I have done. I have frittered away my opportunities like children at the seashore who fill their hands with sand and then let the grains all fall through their open fists. It is not too late for me. I can still fill my hands. I can still shape a future of success and happiness. I am capable of great wonders, and now I know that my achievements will never rise higher than my faith in myself. I have new faith. I was made in the image of God. I was not created to fail. Defeat? Possible. Quit? Never again!

These four positive life choices, available to all at no cost, are merely a small sampling of the myriad of options that are available to you every day. Now that you understand the thought process involved, now that you see how easy it is to separate the wheat from the chaff in your life, now that you have been alerted to the truth that you do have choices all along the way, this listing of our common faults and their cures need go no farther. The world is already too filled with rule books, with "how-to" guides, with seminars and cassettes dispensing secrets of success that are not secrets at all. The last thing you need is another set of principles or exhortations on how to make it big, how to accumulate wealth, how to restore your wandering self-esteem. And if the truth were known, we humans seldom pay much attention to columns of instructions, regulations, laws, and canons, no matter how important or beneficial they may seem. Consider the most important guides for living we have ever received, the Ten Commandments. Even those sacred laws are frequently ignored since less than half of all those who piously profess to believe in them can recite more than five!

And what about happiness, peace of mind, contentment, serenity? If you now choose to raise your sights and reach for success, if you choose to pursue fame and glory, must these all-important qualities of a good life be sacrificed? Are they the terrible price you and your family must always pay, as have so many others, to reach your new goals?

The choice is up to you. Do you want it all—success plus happiness and peace of mind and contentment and serenity? Isn't that too much to expect? No! Open your heart and you will find that it is not difficult. Just choose to live each day as two others of long ago prayed they might live, two others who surely were special messengers of God. Take the time to memorize their humble pleas, combined here only because they seem to have sprung from the same loving heart:

Lord, make me an instrument of your peace;

where there is hatred, let me sow love;

where there is injury, pardon;

where there is doubt, faith;

where there is despair, hope;

where there is darkness, light;

and where there is sadness, joy.

I shall pass through this world but once. Any good therefore that I can do, or any kindness that I can show to any human being, let me do it now. Let me not defer nor neglect it, for I shall not pass this way again.

Now you are free!

At last you can unlock your cell door and walk with head high toward the future you deserve, knowing that God does not require you to live on credit; He pays us what we earn as we earn it, good or evil, heaven or hell, according to our choice.

There is a better way to live . . . and you have discovered the missing key!

Choose to use it!

XXI

I RETURNED TO JAFFREY ON THE DAY AFTER MY YANKEE Stadium appearance completely spent. Drained both emotionally and physically. When I crawled into my own bed, after what had seemed years of absence, I slept for twenty-four hours. And yet, to Louise's amazement, I was back in my beloved Tower of Success just two days later, banging away on this old Underwood, racing to put down my recollections of the events of the past six years before I ran out of days and nights. "No later than the first day of the new year," Alex had warned. Of course, Louise believed that I had commenced work on the next book, motivated by my fresh experiences and encounters during the tour. I did nothing to correct her assumptions.

Writing this entire narrative took fifteen days and was completed on October 18. For what I had planned as the final chapter, Chapter XX, I wrote a few paragraphs about my inability to recall any of the speech, as you have read, attached that page to one of the Goliath newspaper ads featuring *The Key to a Better Life*, placed it all in a folder, and locked the thing away in the bottom file drawer of my desk. *Every chapter that you have read is exactly as I wrote it, and no alterations have been made in light of what has happened since.*

Louise, I am positive, could now sense a change in me. Probably my two sons did also. Although I worked very hard at trying to be the husband and father I always had been, I know I failed miserably. I was moodier, lost my temper for trivial reasons, and the banter that had been such a precious part of the interaction between all of us had just about disappeared. Among themselves they were probably rationalizing my strange behavior, blaming it on the tremendous strain I had been under during the tour. Soon, any day now, Dad would be his old self again.

Each morning I awoke grateful that I had made it through another night and yet that feeling would dissipate quickly to be replaced by the sickening realization that this might be the last day I would ever see the sun or smell the pine trees or listen to the voices of those I loved so very much. Endlessly, I searched through my library in the tower, seeking solace and advice from great minds of the past who had wrestled with the inevitability of death. They were little consolation. I gained no courage in reading that "death is not a foe, but an invisible adventure" or that "death is the golden key that opens the palace of eternity." The only adventure I craved was a walk in the woods with Todd and Glenn, and the only palace I cared about was on a hilltop in Jaffrey.

I became extremely absent-minded—losing mundane things such as car keys and my wallet, forgetting where I had parked when I was downtown, misplacing my favorite pen or the magazine I was reading. Names would crop up in conversations with Louise, and they would mean nothing to me, although I pretended they did. And several times every day and night I would ponder Alexander Anthony's story of the Century Plant. I, too, was about to become a Century Plant. My brief moment of glory had come, and now the tall stalk that had been Mark Christopher was about to crash to earth.

Eventually, my bitterness at the cruel hand that fate was dealing began to fade—or perhaps I just got tired of fighting it, accepting the words of that wise old Roman, Seneca, who wrote, "What must be shall be; and that which is a necessity to him that struggles, is little more than choice to him that is willing." Choice again. But never, at any point, did I allow my fears to tarnish any of the beliefs and principles I had championed in my book regarding man's potential to uplift his life through the proper use of the tools, the gifts he had received from his Creator. My faith in God remained strong. I prayed for help, for the guts to hold together through whatever was ahead. Mr. Success, trying to find his way without his trusty compass.

Thanksgiving arrived. The boys and I watched a football game on television as we had for many years while Louise worked her usual magic in the kitchen. During the following week, Louise and her helpers began to be inundated under an avalanche of Christmas mail, causing her to regretfully postpone our annual holiday shopping binge that she had looked forward to for weeks. I secretly welcomed the delay since I wasn't sure I could handle the happy sights and sounds of Noel in my state of mind. While Louise and the others busily sorted through the greeting cards, searching for letters that needed our attention, I spent more and more time in the tower, alone, waiting . . .

I was sitting at my desk, one day, staring at the calendar, when I decided to burn these pages. It had suddenly occurred to me that my self-serving account of the past would be a terrible legacy to leave to Todd—a wound that would scar him permanently with the knowledge that he was alive only because his father had agreed to trade his own life in order that his son might live. How mindless of me! How blind! I had just unlocked the file drawer where the typescript was stored when Louise rushed into the tower.

"What's the matter, hon?"

Out of breath from running, she gasped, "Here," and handed me a familiar-looking buff-colored envelope on which my name was written in light blue calligraphy. I tore it open and read the message on the gold-bordered card. I read it again. And again.

> *You have not been forsaken.*
>
> *I have interceded in your behalf and wrought my first and last miracle.*
>
> *The schedule has been changed.*
>
> *After long and due deliberation, and with the words of your powerful message still echoing through the infinite hills of paradise, it has been decided that you are to remain as you are, where you are, among those you love, so that you may continue to share, unselfishly, the key to a better life with all humanity.*
>
> *You might also be interested to learn that I was ably assisted in my arguments in your behalf by another fellow writer whose opinion carries much weight, a man named Joshua Croydon.*

May you and your family enjoy a Merry Christmas and many more Happy New Years . . . together.

I stood there so long, just staring at the words, that Louise finally took the card from my hand and read it. She handed it back. "I don't understand, Mark. What does it mean? And this card isn't signed. No A. B. Salom . . . no Absalom."

I grabbed her around the waist and lifted her high above the stone floor. Then I led her to the sofa and told her everything. Everything!

"Oh, my God," she said, again and again. "And you've been carrying that terrible burden around since—since that plane flight from Memphis. Yet you finished the tour, and you made your speech as if everything was okay with your world!"

"I tried, lady, I sure as hell tried."

"It's a wonder you didn't crack up completely. Why didn't you tell me? No, don't answer. I know. You didn't want to dump on me, right?"

For the first time since I had returned from my tour there was the priceless sound of laughter in the tower. Lots of it.

On Christmas day, the very best one of my life, after the last present had been opened I turned to Louise. "How much time do we have before you introduce us to that sweet-smelling turkey you keep basting?"

"Two hours," she said, "give or take fifteen minutes. Why?"

"I'm going to take a drive. Be back in an hour or so, okay?"

"Sure." She cocked her head. "Stoddard?"

"Yes. I want to thank him. Can't think of a better day to do it."

"What makes you think Mr. Anthony will be there? I would think that his 'duties' keep him moving around."

"It's worth a try."

As I was slipping into my topcoat, Louise came into the hall. "Mark, you don't have a present for him. How can you drop in on Christmas without a gift?"

"Oh, gosh, you're right. Any ideas?"

"Yes. Bring Todd. I think the old man will be pleased to meet the other half of the option."

A light snow that had fallen during the evening still clung to the pavement but the road to Stoddard was almost empty of traffic and the trip took less than thirty minutes. I found Birch Point Lane with no difficulty, drove up the narrow dirt road exactly half a mile, as I had on my first visit, and stopped, searching for the opening in the row of blueberry bushes along the road. There was none. Through the maze of leafless branches I could see all the way to the pond. Something was wrong. Something was different.

"Let's get out, Todd."

Together we forced our way through the stubborn wall of interlocking shrubs, and Todd followed as I almost ran down the incline toward a huge fieldstone fireplace that rose like a gray iceberg from a surrounding cluster of young pine and hemlock.

Todd stumbled and fell, clambering to his feet and pointing to the charred beam that had tripped him. "There was a fire here, Daddy, but it must have been a long time ago. Look how tall some of these trees are."

I eased my way between the small saplings until I was standing next to the fireplace and I could feel the hair beginning to rise on the back of my neck. As I was rubbing my hand against the uneven platform of rock that had once held a sturdy mantel, a voice inquired, "Can I help you folks?"

I turned to see an elderly woman wearing a shawl coming toward us. She was supporting herself with a makeshift cane and rocked from side to side with each step. "Merry Christmas," she smiled, waving the cane. "Are ye looking for someone? I live right up the road there, and maybe I can be of assistance."

"Yes," I replied, although my voice sounded strange, "we're looking for Mr. Anthony . . ."

"Who?"

"Anthony. Alexander Anthony. He had a house here, if I'm not mistaken."

"Anthony. Oh sure, he used to live here. All alone. Nice man. Never bothered no one. He passed away in, let's see now, 1964—or was it '65? Had no kin, at least none we ever knew about. The town buried him in our little cemetery back of the church. I went to the funeral, me and Alfred, my husband. He's passed on, too. Alfred and I were the only ones there, at the funeral. Except for the minister. And then, only a week after Mr. Anthony was buried, we had a terrible storm. Lots of lightning. One of the bolts struck his house. Burned it to the ground. A crying shame. All those books inside—nothing but ashes."

"Thank you," I said softly.

She nodded and waved her cane again as she turned away. "Glad to be of service. Merry Christmas!"

"Merry Christmas," Todd shouted at the retreating figure as he moved closer to me, sensing that something was not quite as it should be. "Shall we go now, Dad?"

"I guess we'd better, son."

He walked past the fireplace and kicked at a solitary beam resting against the blackened stones. Then he reached down and picked up a round object burned almost beyond recognition.

"Look, Dad," he cried, rubbing his discovery in the palms of both hands. "It's a baseball! A baseball! And there's writing on it!"

I held out my hand, and he dropped the smoke-stained sphere into it. For several seconds I caressed it before I was finally able to raise it to my eyes and read the only word that was still legible . . .

LOVE

ABOUT THE AUTHOR

OG MANDINO is the most widely read inspirational and self-help author in the world today. His fourteen books have sold more than twenty-five million copies in eighteen languages. Thousands of people from all walks of life have openly credited Og Mandino with turning their lives around and for the miracle they have found in his words. His books of wisdom, inspiration, and love include *A Better Way to Live; The Choice; The Christ Commission; The Gift of Acabar; The Greatest Miracle in the World; The Greatest Salesman in the World; The Greatest Salesman in the World, Part II: The End of the Story; The Greatest Secret in the World; The Greatest Success in the World; Mission: Success!; Og Mandino's University of Success; and The Return of the Ragpicker.*